CARPENTERS

AN ILLUSTRATED DISCOGRAPHY

RANDY L. SCHMIDT

with

Justin Vivian Bond, Michelle Berting Brett, Nath Ann Carrera, Jeffrey de Hart,
Mary Edwards, Gina Garan, Cynthia Gibb, Harriet, Quentin Harrison,
Doug Haverty, Drew Jansen, Richard Tyler Jordan, David Konjoyan, Michael Lansing,
Daniel J. Levitin, Jan McDaniel, Johnny Ray Miller, Tom Nolan, Ted Ottaviano,
Judy Pancoast, Mike Ragogna, Rumer, Joel Samberg, Rob Shirakbari, Tom Smucker,
Paul Steinberg, Patrick Summers, Mark Taft, Chris Tassin, Dena Tauriello,
Gary Theroux, Karen Tongson, and Matt Wallace

A Paul Ashurst Publication

Contents

Introduction

The Carpenters were the top-selling American musical act of the 1970s, crafting love songs that defined a generation. With a trademark sound masterminded by Richard and powered by Karen's distinctive velvety alto, songs like "We've Only Just Begun," "Rainy Days and Mondays," "Superstar," and "Top of the World" elevated the sibling duo to worldwide popularity and eventual record sales of more than 100 million.

Today, some fifty years after their emergence, interest in Carpenters music lives on, as evidenced by the numerous documentaries, tribute acts, and music reissues, including a new album featuring their classic recordings accompanied by the Royal Philharmonic Orchestra and conducted by Richard Carpenter. It's clear that the essence of the Carpenters' appeal remains their recordings. And it is those recordings that we celebrate and explore in this new book.

I enlisted thirty-three diverse and knowledgeable commentators—authors, journalists, musicians, producers, recording industry executives, and other Carpenters enthusiasts—to bring this retrospective to life. Teams of three or four experts were assigned to each album and the listening, planning, and researching commenced. The ensuing discussions with me as moderator were recorded, transcribed, and finessed into the chapters contained herein.

In-depth, insightful, and opinionated, these reviews explore all ten "official" Carpenters studio albums recorded during Karen's lifetime, four posthumous releases of extras and outtakes, a hits compilation, and the solo albums. Contemporaneous reviews and personal reflections from Karen, Richard, and others are also included. It is my hope that, collectively, this material and the selection of images will make *Carpenters: An Illustrated Discography* a cherished part of your collection.

Randy L. Schmidt, 2019

(opposite)
At home in the music room with a copy of *The Ballad of Todd Rundgren*, 1971.

1 OFFERING

Released October 9, 1969
Produced by Jack Daugherty
Recorded at A&M Records, Hollywood, California
Reissued as *Ticket to Ride*

Top Billboard Position: #150

Singles:
"Ticket to Ride" / "Your Wonderful Parade"

by Mary Edwards, Tom Nolan, and Dena Tauriello

The Carpenters' road to A&M Records and eventual superstardom began in New Haven, Connecticut, with the birth of Richard Lynn in 1946 and Karen Anne in 1950. During the summer of 1963, Harold and Agnes Carpenter moved their family to Downey, California, a suburb of Los Angeles, where both kids joined the marching band. It was there that Karen found her calling as a drummer.

The Richard Carpenter Trio was formed in 1965 with its namesake on keyboards, college friend Wes Jacobs on bass (and sometimes tuba), and Karen on drums. The following year, the instrumental jazz group won the annual Battle of the Bands competition at the Hollywood Bowl and landed a short-lived recording contract with RCA-Victor. The trio disbanded when Jacobs left to study classical tuba at Juilliard.

Almost overnight, Karen's husky, rich alto voice emerged and caught the attention of popular session bassist Joe Osborn, who signed her to his Magic Lamp Records label. She recorded several demos

(previous page)
In Hollywood, somewhere off
Highland Avenue, 1969.

Herb Alpert and Jerry Moss,
founders of A&M Records,
at the studio gates, 1416
N. La Brea in Hollywood.

(mostly Richard's original compositions) in Osborn's North Hollywood garage studio during the summer of 1966. One single, "Looking for Love" / "I'll Be Yours," was released but received limited distribution.

While attending Long Beach State, Karen and Richard formed Summerchimes, a vocal quintet comprised of students in Frank Pooler's college choir. By fall of 1967 they were Spectrum, a sextet that played Hoot Nights at the Troubadour and appeared at the Whisky a Go-Go. There was interest from several record labels, including Uni and White Whale, but the group became discouraged and parted ways.

Using Joe Osborn's studio and Spectrum's arrangements, Karen and Richard layered their voices through multitrack overdubbing. Their demo tape reached Herb Alpert, head of A&M Records, and on April 22, 1969, "Carpenters" were signed to the label. Their debut album *Offering* cost $50,000 to make and sold just eighteen thousand units, but the song "Ticket to Ride" became a moderate hit, remaining on the charts for six months and peaking at #54 in April 1970.

SCHMIDT: In the spirit of the album's one-word title, let's each give our own one-word description of the album. I'll start. Experimental.

NOLAN: Ambitious.

EDWARDS: Innovative.

TAURIELLO: Eccentric.

SCHMIDT: Tom, you once called *Offering* "a post-folk soft-psychedelic Southern Californian mini-oratorio." Do those words still ring true to you after all these years?

NOLAN: Good for me! I can see what I was driving at, but I hear it a little differently now, or perhaps a little more objectively. It was a very interesting offering by a group eager to find its own identity, happy to be making music, and drawing on a lot of sounds that were in the air at that time, out here [in Southern California]. And a group in search of its own way of doing things. Whether they saw it that way or not, in retrospect it seems that way.

SCHMIDT: Elements of their signature style are present on *Offering*, but in formative stages. The pairing of Karen's lead vocals on songs like "Someday," "All of My Life," and "Eve" with the

oboe and other reed instruments foreshadows the formula of some of their hits to come. But let's talk about that a cappella choral "Invocation," which opens the album. I smile thinking that the very first sound that came from that very first album was the isolated, unaccompanied voice of Karen.

EDWARDS: The first time I encountered this album, it was truly a religious experience. I listened to Karen Carpenter's voice, that singular voice, and then the combining and layering with Richard. It absolutely gave me the chills. It had an interesting sense of cohesiveness, even though so many tracks from the album have their own discrete narrative. The purest form of who they were and everything that they could possibly accomplish was demonstrated in that album. It went unappreciated when it first came out.

NOLAN: I don't think anyone really heard it or saw it or knew of it. Back then, a hit single was necessary to get any attention for your album. If you didn't have that, an album pretty much went unnoticed, unless someone championed it and really gave it a push.

TAURIELLO: I fell in love immediately with "Someday." That song just wrecks me. That sadness you hear came through in some of those big hits later on. She delivered on those ballads. And to me, on *Offering*, "Someday" is the moment you get that.

NOLAN: "Someday" is the first track on the album where she has the predominant vocal. You just sit up and say, "Whoa! This person is a singer."

TAURIELLO: You can hear that she's a young vocalist. Her voice doesn't sound the same on *Offering* as what she grew into with a little more experience and a better understanding of her instrument. Something was there. There was extraordinary ability and quality. Even in her youth and inexperience, there are moments on that record that give you chills.

SCHMIDT: Dena, you did a wonderful article for *Modern Drummer* in which you wrote about Karen's beginnings as a drummer. Would you share about how she got started, her inspirations, and teachers?

TAURIELLO: Oftentimes we hear of musicians starting as kids, but Karen started late. She didn't really start playing until she was fifteen in the marching band at Downey High School. She was interested in the snare drum, and that led her to a brief stint at Drum City in Hollywood with a private instructor, Bill Douglass. She was a big fan of Joe Morello from the Dave Brubeck Quartet, Ringo Starr, and Buddy Rich. They were all Ludwig artists, incidentally, and she ended up playing Ludwig drums. On *Offering*, you can hear that jazz influence and that Morello-Brubeck jazz feel.

Early A&M Records publicity photo, 1969.

SCHMIDT: There are several songs on *Offering* that reflect what was going on in the world in 1969 in terms of politics, the Vietnam War, and so on. Richard calls "Your Wonderful Parade" an antiestablishment song. Then, of course, there's "Get Together," which was one of the most popular songs of peace from the late 1960s. Any thoughts on these songs?

EDWARDS: I always thought "Your Wonderful Parade" was an impressive account to sum up going against the establishment and calling out convention in a real farcical way. It's funny to think of Carpenters as being angry, but there's an underlying outrage and sarcasm there that I can hear in Richard's voice when he sings, "stand in line, try to climb, meet your wife at cocktail time." They are calling out all these protocols and saying that if this is the way you're going to live your life, you're blind to all the injustices going on around you. To me it was the subtlest of protests.

NOLAN: But the presentation is so jaunty that it's easy to miss and not realize how pointed the lyric is. I am sure they were playing on that contrast, but if the tempo were a little slower, the pointed lyric might sink in. Maybe they were trying to put it in subconsciously.

EDWARDS: It's clearly not a folk song. It has more of a mid-century cinematic feel to it. Like a scene out of *The Graduate*. Dustin Hoffman's character was trying to navigate where he was in the social strata, as well as his future plans, after graduation. I feel like "Your Wonderful Parade" would have been a great song to include in that soundtrack. There's a pushing toward convention and to find something practical. What are you going to do with your life? It's as if Benjamin were speaking the lyrics.

SCHMIDT: Richard provided the lead vocals for five of the songs on *Offering*: **"Your Wonderful Parade," "Get Together," "Turn Away," "What's the Use," "Nowadays Clancy Can't Even Sing." Let's talk about him as a lead vocalist. Tom, what are your thoughts?**

NOLAN: Although Richard had wonderful taste in picking songs, and he and John Bettis became darn good songwriters, I'm not so keen on many of these songs. But it's a fine first presentation. These are good calling cards. Richard has a fine voice and found interesting ways to use it, arrange it, and so on, but if I were listening to that first album as a producer, record company executive, or disc jockey, I'd say focus on the female vocalist. Get that girl front and center and highlight her with wonderful songs. Karen was the dominant presence and should have been featured. They eventually worked out a nice formula including both as vocalists and drawing on Richard's strengths. He picked wonderful material and knew how to showcase Karen within the context of that material.

EDWARDS: When I first heard this album, I was surprised to hear so many tracks with Richard singing lead. I didn't find any of them particularly outstanding until I came across "Nowadays Clancy Can't Even Sing," the Neil Young track. He was at his most energetic. All the others were well intentioned, but "Clancy" brought all his strengths to the core. It's a cool song.

NOLAN: It's so interesting that they would do "Clancy" and some of the other songs. It speaks to their good taste and their interest in some of highly individual songwriters at that time. That's an unusual song. It's interesting, if not gutsy, of Richard to find and do that. And they gave it their own spin. In all these tracks, the non-originals, they sort of go out of their way to do their own arrangements. They alter the melodies, the approach, and the tempos to make them their own. Whether it succeeds or not or whether you agree with their choices, you must note their creativity and originality.

SCHMIDT: Dena, would you speak to the challenges of being a "girl drummer" in those days and what Karen must have faced to play her instrument?

TAURIELLO: There are those moments where people are standing there waiting for you to impress them because they can't believe a girl could play the instrument. And when you do, you get comments like "Oh, you hit hard for a girl" or "You're pretty good for a girl." There was always the qualifying statement of "for a girl."

Karen was a pioneer for me, so it had to be even a little trickier for her. I understand the reason Richard and their

THE CARPENTERS HAVE MADE A THING OF BEAUTY

And the people you sell records to like beautiful things.
They like "Ticket To Ride" by the Carpenters (A & M 1142).
So they're buying it. And more radio stations are playing it.
And that's good. Because it's a beautiful record.
From their first album, "Offering"
(SP 4205). Which is also beautiful. Very.
Music by Richard and Karen Carpenter.
Produced by Jack Daugherty.

REVIEWS

"Brother and sister Richard and Karen Carpenter have come up with fresh and original concepts of music and singing in this debut LP on A&M. Richard's songs and arrangements, especially the overdubbing of his and Karen's voices, combine the best elements of pop, folk-rock, and jazz, and their version of the now classic 'Get Together' makes it sound very new. With radio programming support, Carpenters should have a big hit on their hands."
—*Billboard*

"This album should be bought for 'Ticket to Ride' . . . the most beautiful version of [the song] ever made, stunningly sung by Karen . . . and a couple of others. Just ignore the rest. Whatever you do, keep your eye out for their next album. This is the kind of talent that refines itself quickly."
—*High Fidelity*

"The music of Carpenters' *Offering* isn't geared to any particular age group. Richard shows tremendous versatility in varying tempos and meters, and all of the works feature impeccable harmony. Karen's voice is most often featured, and with good reason. She, too, is versatile, ranging from the blues style, which has recently returned to popularity, to light, happy tunes and background."
—*Southeast Daily News* (Los Angeles, CA)

REFLECTIONS

The Carpenters sound is rock, folk, jazz, pop, soft, this, that, and the other thing.
—Richard (1969)

That album, I had finished in my mind years before we got the contract. That wasn't where I was at the time we signed, and some of it could have been a lot better, but you can hear that the ideas were there. Time-signature changes, extended solos, and things that we don't do now. I should've just forgotten it and gotten down to where I was at the moment. But it was like I had to do that album, I didn't care if we had gotten signed in 1980, that was what the first album was going to sound like.
—Richard (1975)

On our first album, we sang much differently; Karen sang a lot harder in the early days than she does now, and I did too. The drums were far busier on the first album than they are now, and I hear a lot of little things that we've changed since then.
—Richard (1976)

"Ticket to Ride" was kind of a half-hit/half-flop. In some places it was #1, and in other places it was ashtray material.
—Karen (1978)

We were immediately given the run of the entire place. Herb never told Richard anything about a budget. I think we were one of the first ones that ever tried to stuff 50 people into Studio A. I remember we walked in and you couldn't even see. It was just a wall of people.
—Karen (1981)

Something about Karen's voice turned me on immediately— the feeling of her voice—and it felt like her voice was sitting in my lap and like she was in the room. She had a larger-than-life voice.
—Herb Alpert, A&M Records cofounder (1985)

For a debut album by a young act, Offering *is not too shabby. It certainly is filled with a spirit of musical adventure and exemplifies my assimilation of the many styles of music surrounding me while growing up.*
—Richard (1986)

The first album did exactly what I thought it was going to do. It takes a while for people to get onto a new artist and the frequency and the message that they are trying to send out. It didn't surprise me that the public didn't take to it. It was just a matter of time before they found the right song at the right moment and things turned around.
—Herb Alpert (1994)

It's different than what follows because I was a bit of a thickhead. We were so excited to be signed, but we were a bit full of ourselves. A lot of what's on Offering, *John and I wrote for Spectrum back in '67. No one actually sat us down and said, "Now, listen. What is it that you think you're going to be recording?" No one said, "Well, no, I don't think so" or "Why don't you listen to a few demos?" or "Why don't you try to write something new?" No one said anything!*
—Richard (2001)

It's creative, there's a lot of great vocal work, and one of the best things about it is it's so much a product of its time. It's so very Sixties—experimental pop music.
—Richard (2009)

Polaroid taken in the office of *Record World* while in New York City to appear on *Your All-American College Show*, late 1969.

management wanted her to get out from behind the drums and front the group. The lead singer should be seen in that way. But I just wonder if part of it wasn't because the idea of a girl playing the drums. It could be a novelty or a drawing point, but it could be a detriment. I wonder if that might have been part of the equation, in some small way.

SCHMIDT: Karen is said to have recorded the bass guitar parts on "All of My Life" and "Eve." Do you agree that she went against the grain of femininity and the expectations for young ladies?

TAURIELLO: Against the grain and definitely out of the norm. I wish I had a dollar for every person who says to me "Oh, Karen Carpenter was a drummer?" They still don't know that she drummed. But there was no intention there. It wasn't like she was trying to make a statement, she was just trying to make music.

EDWARDS: The unintentional feminist. She wanted to do these things, and she was very good at them. Throughout Western music history, women who chose to be instrumentalists were considered nonconventional, and thereby remained hidden in plain view. Twenty years before the Carpenters, there were women leading big bands. We were not as familiar with Lil Hardin Armstrong as we were Benny Goodman. Karen's strengths, like those of the women musicians before her, gave fortitude to move through what was prescribed.

NOLAN: They were both so incredibly talented and were encouraged by their family and teachers to do all kinds of things. It is wonderful that they found ways to channel these talents and combine them so effectively and so successfully.

SCHMIDT: The obvious gem of *Offering* lies at the start of side two. "Ticket to Ride" was not the first Beatles song that Richard gave this ballad formula. When they were recording in Joe Osborn's garage they cut "Nowhere Man" in almost the same manner. It surfaced many years later as part of the *As Time Goes By* collection. What made "Ticket to Ride" work so beautifully when given this treatment?

EDWARDS: It's far more forlorn than the original Beatles version. It's a sad song. I feel as if the Beatles version almost sounds dismissive, but in this version there's a longing.

NOLAN: The switch of the genders in the lyric makes a big difference, too. And the vocalist. It's such a thrill to hear her cut loose on this song in her very melodic way. Perhaps the familiarity of the song helps, too. You're very aware of the contrast right away. You're drawn to the song because you know it. But the Carpenters' version is just incredible. It's such an appealing cut. Sounds like a hit to me!

EDWARDS: It's also where you get that first real taste of what would become a successful formula. That standard Carpenters arrangement with the use of the oboe. Even though so many songs on side one are equally lush and beautiful, their signature comes forth on "Ticket to Ride." It's as if they finally found their footing on that arrangement.

TAURIELLO: That sort of foreshadowing of Richard's ability to make the arrangement work exactly for them and for Karen. I love the use of the minor chords he puts in there, to give it that sadness.

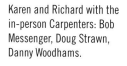

Karen and Richard with the in-person Carpenters: Bob Messenger, Doug Strawn, Danny Woodhams.

NOLAN: To make a Beatles song your own is impressive. "Ticket" is immediately likeable. You want to hear more from these people. It's another example of their ability to put their own stamp on things and their willingness to change the harmonies a little bit and make the song their own.

SCHMIDT: Right. And to not just cover the song. How about the ending and that lush, four-part harmony coda or tag with them singing, "Think I'm gonna be sad." This sort of foreshadows the "wah" ending on "Close to You." Mary, does this feel a little Bacharach inspired to you?

EDWARDS: It does, especially when you get into that modal breakdown. They took a cue from the Bacharach/David catalog with the melodies, colorizations, and other things you wouldn't normally hear on a commercial pop song. And that was the success for them.

SCHMIDT: "Don't Be Afraid" was one of my first favorite Carpenters songs. It was certainly a product of its time, but there's such an unfettered joy that shines through on that one. What are your favorites and why?

EDWARDS: "All I Can Do" is such a lovely standout. It's unlike anything that they did after the first album. I just love how it almost doesn't even fit with the sequence, yet I'm so grateful that it's there. Wonderful and complex.

NOLAN: "All I Can Do" features Richard's keyboard work and it reminds me a little bit of what was to come from Ray Manzarek and the Doors. At one point it almost sounded like he was going to go into the solo for "Riders on the Storm." It certainly harkens back to their jazz trio, which I remember seeing on television when they were in that Hollywood Bowl contest they won. It was so extraordinary to see these guys and a girl drummer. As I recall, they were the only group playing jazz in this competition. And then they won. They were the outstanding act and so full of enthusiasm and talent.

TAURIELLO: It's obvious that *Offering* was a transitional album. They were still somewhere between the jazz feel of the Richard Carpenter Trio and the pop act they ultimately became. It's very evident in Karen's drumming, which was a lot busier style and more of a jazz approach than traditional pop. It's incredibly impressive, though, especially considering she had been drumming for all of about four years at that point. To be able to do a lot of what she was doing on that record is remarkable. You can really hear the subtleties, nuances, and technical ability. That isn't always as evident in a straight-up pop song. It's a tremendous showcase for her ability.

2 CLOSE TO YOU

Released August 19, 1970
Produced by Jack Daugherty
Recorded at A&M Studios, Hollywood, CA

Top Billboard Position: #2

RIAA Certification: 2x Multiplatinum

Singles:
"(They Long to Be) Close to You" / "I Kept on Loving You"
"We've Only Just Begun" / "All of My Life"

with Mike Ragogna, Rumer, and Rob Shirakbari

The three Bs—The Beach Boys, the Beatles, and Burt Bacharach—were the major influences on the early Carpenters sound. In December 1969, Bacharach invited Karen and Richard to be his opening act and asked them to arrange and perform a medley of his songs written with Hal David. It was during the construction of that medley that Richard was introduced to a seven-year-old song that would change everything.

As the in-person Carpenters group rehearsed tirelessly on A&M's soundstage, Herb Alpert stopped by and suggested "They Long to Be Close to You," a lesser-known Bacharach-David song recorded by Richard Chamberlain and Dionne Warwick. Although it was not right for the medley, the lead sheet sat on Richard's Wurlitzer for several weeks, and he started to see its potential as a stand-alone song.

Within just two months of its release, the Carpenters' version of "(They Long to Be) Close to You" was in the #1 spot on the Hot 100, where it stayed for four weeks, and quickly sold two million copies. The

(previous page)
Photographed in the
graphics department at
A&M, July 8, 1970.

follow up was "We've Only Just Begun," a Roger Nichols–Paul Williams tune Richard discovered in a TV commercial for Crocker Bank. Released alongside the *Close to You* album in August 1970, "Begun" peaked at #2 on the Hot 100.

With three gold records—the "Close to You" single, *Close to You* album, and "We've Only Just Begun"—the Carpenters were the hottest recording act in America. By December 1970, their appearance fee jumped from two figures to five, and their first royalty check was for $50,000. Karen, Richard, and their parents soon moved into a sprawling home at 9828 Newville Avenue in Downey. Other investments included two apartment houses they named "Close to You" and "Only Just Begun."

The first major recognition for the Carpenters within the music industry came on the evening of March 16, 1971, at the Thirteenth Annual Grammy Awards. Nominated in five categories, they won for Best New Artist and Best Contemporary Performance by a Duo, Group, or Chorus, a category in which they were nominated alongside the Jackson Five, Simon and Garfunkel, Chicago, and the Beatles.

SCHMIDT: The album opens with "We've Only Just Begun," which was originally written as a bank commercial and soon became the Carpenters' signature tune. Richard had a knack for discovering songs in the most unusual places and taking good songs and making them great, wouldn't you say?

RUMER: Absolutely. That was characteristic of them as a band. They found these diamonds in the rough, polished them up, and made them their own.

Performing on *The Don Knotts Show*, 1970.

RAGOGNA: We know the roots and history of that song ad nauseam, but "We've Only Just Begun" was a metaphor for many things. They kicked off their career with "Close to You," their first huge hit, but "We've Only Just Begun" solidified it. In a way, "Begun" launched their career as their continuation of hits.

SHIRAKBARI: As formed and defined as they were on their first record, *Offering*, the production on *Close to You* is sonically amazing. Near perfect. This album jumps out and says, "We are fully formed." Sonically, they'd hit that spot. And the template that was established with "We've Only Just Begun" carried on through their whole career.

RUMER: On *Offering* they were finding their sound and it was more in a classical vein, whereas on this record they're harnessing the woodwinds and strings. Their signature sound was that combination of Karen's voice, the arrangements, the woodwinds, and so on. It all came together to crystallize that pop sound.

RAGOGNA: *Close to You* was such a giant leap. *Offering* didn't hint that *Close to You* was coming.

SHIRAKBARI: The album wasn't finished when the single came out, so the massive success of the "Close to You" single really lit a fire under them and forced them into that prolific period. Everything fell into place from that.

RAGOGNA: When I was in the sixth grade, a classmate brought the *Close to You* album and played it during a free period, and it caught everybody's attention. The kids stopped everything they were doing and just listened!

SHIRAKBARI: That's interesting, because there was the critical slam against them at the time for being out of step with all the heavy stuff going on in the world at the time. But to a kid in sixth grade, they're not going to be embracing the full impact of the Vietnam War.

RAGOGNA: Right. You don't even know what that is.

RUMER: If a child can have a pure response to something, you know that it touches the heart.

RAGOGNA: It's like it trained a generation on how to listen. Purity attracted purity.

SCHMIDT: Few people know that "Love Is Surrender" began its life as a contemporary Christian song with the lyric "Love is surrender to His will."

SHIRAKBARI: Ralph Carmichael was a legend in that contemporary Christian world. I was involved in that when I was a kid through the church I was in and was familiar with his body of work. The lyric changes secularized it but retained the spirit.

RUMER: It wasn't unusual for church music to be adapted as pop music. It had been done for many years. I love that they put their own

spin on this devotional song and it kept that devotional quality. It uplifts the spirit in the same way as a devotional song or a hymn.

SCHMIDT: "Maybe It's You" is one of several Carpenter/Bettis tunes that dates to 1968 and their vocal group Spectrum.

SHIRAKBARI: If you think that "We've Only Just Begun" is a fluke and if "Love Is Surrender" isn't your thing, you realize that Richard as an arranger and producer is a force when you get to "Maybe It's You." It's on full display here in terms of the beauty of the song, the recording, and the arrangement.

RUMER: And Karen's voice. Richard told me they sang *really* close to the mic. Engineers say you shouldn't sit so close to the mic, but the Carpenters deliberately sang close to the mic. It may have been an unconventional recording method, but it communicated her message through the speakers in a very penetrating way.

RAGOGNA: That is my favorite Carpenters song ever. When I was a kid, I heard it playing on an old stereo in a Hadassah furniture store and it felt like a phenomenon. Again, it seemed like everyone was listening to that song and the store got quieter as it played. Something about it grabs you. You have no choice!

SCHMIDT: Karen and Richard had been performing Tim Hardin's "Reason to Believe" for several years by this point. Is there anything that particularly sets their version apart from others?

SHIRAKBARI: They had a nose for good songs. This was the year before Rod Stewart's version was the B-side of "Maggie May" and *Every Picture Tells a Story* was huge. There is very little guitar on Carpenters records, but if you listen to the way Richard plays the Wurli, it could almost be a guitar part.

RAGOGNA: The Wurlitzer is a great part. And if you heard the Tim Hardin or Rod Stewart versions after hearing the Carpenters version, you'd think the others were demos in comparison to what the Carpenters did with that record.

RUMER: Tim Hardin was a favorite of many bands. A lot of musicians respected and loved him. He was a fragile guy, and there was a fragility in his writing and a vulnerability to him. Karen and Richard probably enjoyed and picked up on that.

SCHMIDT: "Help" was one in a string of Beatles songs reimagined by the Carpenters. They'd done their own interpretation of "Nowhere Man" in Joe Osborn's garage studio, recorded "Can't Buy Me Love" for the *Navy Presents* radio program, and released "Ticket to Ride" as their debut single. I use the term reimagined because they never just "covered" a Beatles song.

REVIEWS

"Karen and Richard Carpenter have taken the music world by storm with their beautiful 'Close to You' million-seller, and they are on their way to repeating that success with their current 'We've Only Just Begun.' Their smooth blend of voices is evident throughout this LP, which includes both those hits and they should skyrocket up the bestselling album charts. Another gem is their treatment of 'Baby It's You.'"
—*Billboard*

"The combined talents of the Carpenters are irresistible. Richard is the axis; from the sound of things he works ferociously—hundreds of hours must have gone into this album. . . . The other part of this winning combination is Karen Carpenter's voice, warmly innocent, full and dark and deep. . . . She has several distinct voices—one is the now familiar solo voice; the others are used to create layers of vocal chorus."
—*High Fidelity*

"Squeaky-clean, that's what the Carpenters are. They look just like your average young pop-music-millionaire kids next door, and they sing just about the way you'd expect a smooth commercial entity would. That is, not too loud, not too fast, not too funky—and not too interesting. . . . I know that there is a huge audience for this sort of middle-America hokum and that every few years a new set of juveniles and ingenues come along to persuade the old folks that young folks are just as upstanding as ever."
—*Stereo Review*

REFLECTIONS

Our first album had 10 originals, but I've got to be objective. I like my original material very much and yet if "Close to You" comes up and says, "Hi, I'm 'Close to You,'" I gotta say, "Hi, you're a hit," and put aside my pride and put it out.
—**Richard (1970)**

I think the greatest thing that's happened so far is having the number-one record in the country, having it go over two million records, and have it be the biggest single that A&M Records ever had. I think that's the greatest feeling in the world.
—**Karen (1970)**

It's not only taken us by surprise, I think it's part shock, too. We always hoped to have a hit record, but for it to happen to that extent, even for it to happen, is beyond your sight. All I know is that it's made us two happy people. How could it help but do that? It's outasight!
—**Karen (1970)**

When "Close to You" came out, it seemed that the public was ready for it . . . People again want nice, simple, nostalgic, romantic things. I think that hard rock slipped when Janis Joplin and Jimi Hendrix died. Psychologically, their deaths had something to do with it. Even many of the kids were turned away from hard rock and are listening to softer, sweeter things.
—**Richard (1971)**

Some press photos and album covers I can stomach, as far as sending 'em out with the press kits. But I'm still waiting for something that really knocks me out. And some, especially that Close to You *cover . . . zero imagination. . . .*

When they brought it in I said, "I don't like it." They said, "Learn to love it." I have never learned to love it. I hate it.
—**Richard (1974)**

We put out our first record and it did OK. It went to #56 in the country, but it stuck around for about six months. It wouldn't die and it wouldn't go all the way. It kept hangin' in there. And in the midst of this whole thing we found "Close to You" and when we released that, that was #1 in six weeks, so it was like instant overnight success that took three years.
—**Karen (1981)**

It's hard to predict that type of success. Their success was just beyond it all. We're always looking for artists who can go over the centerfield fence, but they really went beyond that. They went over the third deck!
—**Herb Alpert (1985)**

The Carpenters were truly one of the first great alternative bands. "In-A-Gadda-Da-Vida" was the huge #1 album shortly before "Close to You" and "Begun" were hits. I was so different from them, too. I was such a raging hippie. I was pretty much a part of the counterculture yet writing songs for Karen and Richard and a lot of other middle-of-the-road acts.
—**Paul Williams, composer (2002)**

If looked at objectively, the Carpenters saved the label because 1969 was not a good period for A&M. . . . If you look at the charts, there was not a #1 single on A&M for two years, almost to the month. "This Guy's In Love with You" in 1968 and "Close to You" in 1970. It was a rough patch.
—**Richard (2014)**

Karen chats with young fans during a sound check at the University Gymnasium, Cal State.

RAGOGNA: My feeling is that this was aimed at being a single. It just has the feel of that to me.

SHIRAKBARI: The key to a successful cover is that you make it sound like your own song. And it's very hard to yank that away from the Beatles. There's a desperation to the lyric that comes through on the original Beatles version that just isn't there for me on this one. This is the only outlier on this album.

SCHMIDT: This album exhibits a lot of Bacharach influence before we even come to "(They Long to Be) Close to You." Let's talk about Richard's arrangement here and what it took for this little-known Bacharach/David tune to become #1-hit material.

RAGOGNA: This was unlike *anything* else on radio, which speaks to Richard's brilliance. And this was recorded from a lead sheet? That is a pretty wild "something from nothing" adventure.

SHIRAKBARI: Burt is on record saying he missed the mark on his arrangement for "Close to You" with the slow ballad approach. He gives Richard full credit for popularizing that song. And the "wah" section at the end was Richard's nod to Bacharach. It recalls how Burt would sometimes finish a song and then add an instrumental interlude. Sometimes it would be a new composition, like what comes in at the end of "Raindrops Keep Fallin' on My Head." That's very Bacharach.

RUMER: Theirs was a sound that no one had really heard before. The essence of who they were was in the DNA of every song. It was truly them. People were hearing Karen and Richard—the artists—and not some record company construct.

RAGOGNA: This was a major signpost for pop music. It announced that you were about to embark on an interesting journey. And following up with "We've Only Just Begun" just cemented this journey that everyone was on called "Carpenters."

SCHMIDT: Let's flip to side two, which begins with "Baby It's You," another Bacharach composition and perhaps one of the most underrated of those early Carpenters tunes. Rumer, why do you think Karen's voice was so perfectly suited to sing Bacharach?

RUMER: Karen was a storyteller and had a great respect for the composition. There was a willingness to tell the story in the purest

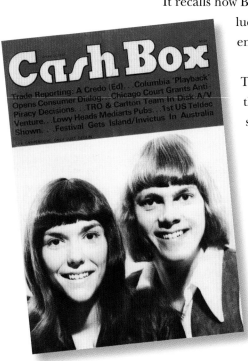

possible form. Bacharach writes very specifically and with notes that need to ring out. And her voice rang out like a bell.

SHIRAKBARI: "Baby It's You" is a very Carpenters-sounding arrangement of a Bacharach song. Again, the gold standard of a great cover is to make it sound like you wrote it. And on this one, everything is there that makes a good Carpenters record: the high bass line, the oboe, the way the vocals are arranged. They really reimagined this one to great effect. The Shirelles version was great, as was the one Elvis did. A lot of people have done this song, but the Carpenters made it a Carpenters song.

SCHMIDT: The Bacharach train keeps chugging along with "I'll Never Fall in Love Again," a recording Richard often cited as having the most voices on it. It's apparently a thirteen-part, thirty-nine-voice chord at the layered "here to remind you" part.

SHIRAKBARI: What's amazing is that this was all done with sixteen-track recording. This was an indicator of where things were going in the future. That's dense. To get that much density out of sixteen tracks there had to be a lot of submixing and bouncing going on. That's really pushing it for those times.

In concert at Cal State Long Beach, December 1970.

Attending the 13th Annual Grammy Awards, March 16, 1971, where they won Best New Artist and Best Contemporary Vocal Performance by a Duo.

RAGOGNA: This was right around the time that Todd Rundgren and other producers were starting to look at that. Roy Thomas Baker had to have listened to and digested what was going on.

SHIRAKBARI: This was pre-Queen and years ahead of *A Night at the Opera* and *A Day at the Races*. Technologically, the Carpenters were really pushing the boundaries in constructing that big magical sound of theirs. They were at the front end of this.

RAGOGNA: It was the formative years for those producers. How could they escape this music? Whether they liked it or not, they picked up on all of it and these producers were using a Carpenters technique.

RUMER: They didn't get enough credit. Karen was a lot more collaborative in the studio than women would normally be during that time. As a female in a recording studio, you're not really asked for your opinion, but when I had the honor of working with Richard, I genuinely felt that he was interested in my opinion. This led me to muse that Karen was perhaps as involved in the production decisions as he was.

SHIRAKBARI: I was told that Hal Blaine, the Wrecking Crew session drummer, has said that for some of the recordings he played on they would run them down with Karen playing first. That means a lot of the approach and form was already established by her playing. He would then interpret that through the ears and experience of a seasoned session drummer.

RUMER: I have a sense that perhaps Karen was as integral as Richard was in terms of the overall production. It's likely that he sought out her opinion.

RAGOGNA: Which makes sense, because we eventually saw her credited as associate producer. He wouldn't just randomly hand out that credit.

SCHMIDT: "Crescent Noon" has always been a favorite of mine. It reminds me more of an art song than a pop song. What are your opinions of it?

RAGOGNA: This was a perfect choral piece. It sounds like one of those mandatory pieces for every college choir. The lyrics are so syllabic, and it's one of the most beautiful vocal arrangements I've ever heard.

SCHMIDT: Victor Guder was the entertainment supervisor at Disneyland in the summer of 1967 when John Bettis and Richard were the banjo-piano act at Coke Corner on Main Street U.S.A. The song "Mr. Guder" was named for him and contains some interesting classical influences, both choral and instrumental.

RAGOGNA: I've heard that Richard regrets having written this song. He feels it was impetuous youth and too much of a slam on the real Mr. Guder.

RUMER: Of the two of them, I'm sure John Bettis was the ringleader! Richard's a very respectful guy, extremely polite, and pure hearted, so I imagine him being uncomfortable with that. But I can see a young John writing those lyrics.

RAGOGNA: It took two to tango, though. Richard didn't exactly pull it from the record. But it's a great arrangement, especially the section that sounds like something from the Swingle Singers. This would have been one of the first introductions to that sound on a major pop record.

SCHMIDT: My favorite of all Richard's vocal performances is "I Kept on Loving You." The Williams/Nichols tune was briefly considered as the A-side for "Close to You," which would have been a mistake, but it's clearly a great song for him.

SHIRAKBARI: I love this. Richard's vocal on this sounds like he's in the '60s, which they were just coming out of, but it's also of the '70s. And it sounds like a precursor to what would happen years later with Seals and Croft, England Dan and John Ford Coley, and there's even that John Sebastian vibe. It sounds like a TV theme and really bridges that gap from the '60s to the '70s.

RAGOGNA: That's my favorite vibe for Richard Carpenter. You can picture him in that jacket with a turtleneck and the whole look. It seems like this was the first time Richard really stepped out. His identity was clear for that moment.

SHIRAKBARI: There's a confidence in this performance that makes it cut through. It's a fun track to listen to. He could have been on his way to having a solo career with this record in different circumstances.

SCHMIDT: The album closes with "Another Song," another Spectrum-era tune that begins with a baroque-sounding recitative but then kicks off into a majestic and wonderful instrumental passage. Apart from the last minute or so of "Nowadays Clancy Can't Even Sing" on *Offering*, this is unlike anything else they did before or after.

SHIRAKBARI: There's a progressive streak, and you could tell they had big ears and listened to a lot of stuff. You see those little snippets through all their records. There was always something that was a little progressive and this is it on this record.

RAGOGNA: Even though it's very well arranged and succinct, it also feels loose and almost improvisational.

SHIRAKBARI: There's so much cool flute on this recording. There's a Jethro Tull thing going on, and it's maybe even a precursor to Firefall and bands like that where you get the flute as a lead instrument. Like Rumer said earlier, the woodwinds are prominent and a great characteristic of these records.

There was a specific sound to the rooms and the chambers where these records were cut at A&M Studios. The quality standard was getting high with those custom-built Holzer consoles and with Bernie Grundman doing the mastering.

RAGOGNA: In a lot of ways, what the Carpenters were doing became the prototype for A&M Records. Like a flagship; this was not just the Carpenters sound, it was the A&M sound.

3 CARPENTERS

Released May 14, 1971
Produced by Jack Daugherty
Recorded at A&M Studios, Hollywood, CA

Top Billboard Position: #2

RIAA Certification: 4x Multiplatinum

Singles:
"For All We Know" / "Don't Be Afraid"
"Rainy Days and Mondays" / "Saturday"
"Superstar" / "Bless the Beasts and
Children"

with Richard Tyler Jordan, Jan McDaniel, and
Matt Wallace

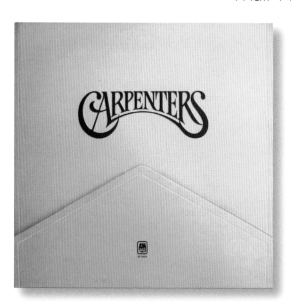

The self-titled *Carpenters* album (*The Tan Album*) was the first of a string of their releases to "ship gold," which at the time indicated presales of more than a million copies. No longer an opening act, Karen and Richard were full-fledged headliners performing for capacity crowds at Carnegie Hall, the Hollywood Bowl, and a one-nighter at the Ohio State Fair for a crowd of fifty thousand, their largest audience ever.

In many ways, this third album signified the duo's arrival, which was represented visually with the new stylized logo embossed in a rich brown across the cover. Designed by Craig Braun, Inc., the insignia drew attention to their official name of Carpenters, sans prefix. The gatefold "envelope" album design was unique in that it converted into an antique-style freestanding frame.

As hosts of *Make Your Own Kind of Music*, their own eight-episode summer replacement series on NBC-TV, Karen and Richard welcomed

(previous page)
Publicity portrait for the
NBC-TV's *Make Your Own
Kind of Music*, 1971.

(right)
Karen, 1971.

Outside the Newville
house with Richard's 1971
Maserati Ghibli.

a variety of popular music guests, including Mac Davis, Jose Feliciano, Anne Murray, Helen Reddy, Dusty Springfield, B. J. Thomas, and the Fifth Dimension. Despite the publicity value, the Carpenters' first encounter with television was mishandled and left them frustrated. It would be another five years before they agreed to host another television show.

The summer of 1971 brought an end to Karen's role as the group's primary drummer in live appearances. Taking cues from the critics, Richard and the duo's managers felt Karen's drums were in the way and disconnecting her from the audience. Karen put up a strong fight, but finally agreed on a plan to drum on some of their uptempo numbers but step out front and center to sing the ballads.

Peaking at #2 on the *Billboard* album chart, *Carpenters* remained in the Top 10 for six months. It spawned three million-selling singles, "For All We Know," "Rainy Days and Mondays," and "Superstar," all of which went Top 3 on the *Hot 100* and #1 on the Adult Contemporary chart. In the end, "For All We Know" won the Oscar for Best Original Song and *The Tan Album* earned three Grammy nominations and won for Best Pop Vocal Performance by a Group.

SCHMIDT: When I first picked up *The Tan Album*, I thought it was most likely a "greatest hits" collection, because there were so many big-name songs included. It was also the album that debuted the Carpenters logo that is so recognizable. Is there another album that more perfectly defines the Carpenters and their sound?

MCDANIEL: It's a toss-up between this album and *A Song for You*, which was similarly packed with hits. I haven't done an actual count to see, but those two represent the golden era. *The Tan Album* was the first album I bought. I remember feeling that the presentation of the album was as special as the production of the music.

WALLACE: *The Tan Album* was the album that got me into the Carpenters and helped me to become a fan, more than just a cursory listener on the radio. This one really connected with me. It was the moment where I really opened my eyes and said, "Wow, this is something special."

JORDAN: This album is certainly one of their finest. It was the first time I found an album by a pop group where I felt every track could have been a hit.

So many artists or groups would simply put out a disc where they had their one hit and everything else was filler. I felt the arrangements on the tan album were brilliant and every song was worthy of airplay.

By the pool with their dogs, Mush and Lady, 1971.

SCHMIDT: The team of Roger Nichols and Paul Williams wrote the opening track, "Rainy Days and Mondays." This was submitted to them shortly after the enormous success of "We've Only Just Begun," another Williams/Nichols tune.

JORDAN: It's the most melancholy song and was simply made for Karen's rich and soulful voice. There's that ever so slight hitch in her voice at the very end and I always wait for it. It's on the word "down" when she sings the final "Rainy days and Mondays always get me down."

MCDANIEL: It's a little dip in pitch, yes. The song's placement as first on side one of the LP was perfect. It also marks the formulation of what I call Richard's ballad arrangement formula: a wind instrument with piano for the intro, in this case a harmonica, and the strings coming in during the second A section, the "sweetening." The backup vocals are delayed until the end of the bridge. It's quite a long time

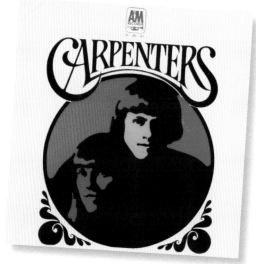

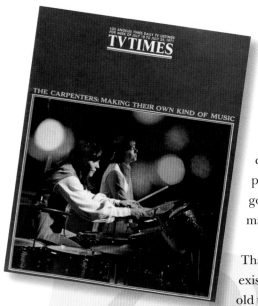

with just Karen's voice, so it gives a chance to express almost the entire song with her alone.

This became Richard's standard formula, and it was a perfect way to showcase Karen's voice in a ballad by having everything else just follow an expected pattern. When a new ballad came out, it made us all feel like we knew what was going to happen. We could just focus on listening to her presentation of the material.

WALLACE: Karen was just twenty when she sang "Rainy Days and Mondays." That's stunning for a woman that young who'd probably led a relatively sheltered existence. Obviously, there was some family turmoil there, but for a twenty-year-old to deliver that song with that kind of nuance, both emotionally and technically, is just stunning. She was the Adele of her time and even beyond that, Karen had more range than Adele does. Adele's fantastic, but Karen really had tremendous pain that went beyond romantic pain as a subtext. Richard's arrangements sometimes made things a bit too big and glossy, but it was Karen's voice and her emotions that punched through all that stuff and said, "This is real."

MCDANIEL: This is the album when Karen really came into her own. There was a lot of rawness in her sound on *Offering* when she was feeling her way through and was still developing. And *Close to You* has some incredible performances, but it also had what I would call plain-sounding, early Karen performances. But her voice on this album is full and every single performance of hers is the Karen that became the voice of the emotional ballad.

SCHMIDT: The first of two Richard leads on the record, "Saturday," is next. It was also one of several Carpenter/Bettis collaborations dating back to 1967 and their days as Spectrum.

WALLACE: Putting "Saturday" in the second slot on this album was a big mistake when you've got "Let Me Be the One," "For All We Know," and "Superstar," which are by far better songs. To put a clunker as number two doesn't make any sense artistically or commercially. Karen can take a mediocre song and elevate it by her singing. Richard, even with the best song, just isn't good enough to draw me in.

MCDANIEL: I have a tender affection for "Saturday." Richard had a pronounced sibilance when he sang and when he spoke. He wrote a song that said, "Saturday began just the same as other days but ended up different in many ways." About as many S-words as you can stack into a song. It was an endearing song. And there is a perfect transition from the end of "Saturday" into "Let Me Be the One" on this album that you don't get to experience in any way other than to listen to this album as it was originally sequenced. It was set up so that the dead space between those two tracks was exactly in tempo to make the downbeat of "Let Me Be the

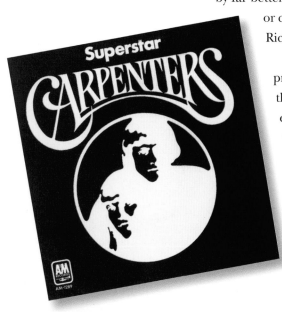

In rehearsal at the Hollywood Bowl, July 16, 1971.

One," which has no introduction. It was a direct segue. I was so fascinated that this minute-and-thirty-second song was not long enough for me to be bothered by it.

SCHMIDT: Speaking of "Let Me Be the One," that was another Williams/Nichols tune that could have been a hit single.

MCDANIEL: "Let Me Be the One" has a brass section. It's a wonderful arrangement that takes the special rhythmic features written into it by Nichols and Karen capitalizes on all of those, making it quite different than "Rainy Days and Mondays" and the other ballads on this album. That's a tough thing to do because there are inherent similarities between Williams/Nichols songs, especially their ballads. This is also the first time on this album where Karen's lead vocal is doubled. That became more and more frequent as they evolved in their production.

WALLACE: They did that to bolster the chorus. It's a fantastic effect, singular Karen vocals on the verses and then doubled in the choruses.

SCHMIDT: Another song that dates to Spectrum is "(A Place to) Hideaway," which they heard performed by Randy Sparks at his Ledbetter's club.

In rehearsal for their
BBC television special,
September 25, 1971.

At the drums, late 1971.

WALLACE: This is just an OK song, and it really feels like an album track to me. I don't think it brings a whole lot to the table. The vocals are good, but it doesn't have that Carpenters spark.

MCDANIEL: It had some awkward moments and the harmonic track it takes at the bridge is peculiar. It's intentionally trying to blaze new ground and is not necessarily successful in doing so. Richard overproduced this one a bit, probably to make up for what he thought were deficiencies in the material. The arrangement has lots of things to give it a bit more character and gravitas. Also, it ends with one of those "happy chords," as I call them. It's an unexpected shift to a major chord on that last note of the song and was a cliché on a lot of early 1970s ballads.

JORDAN: It's a fantastic ballad that really showcases her voice. The lyrics are so hokey, though. "I run through the mist of the wine." I get a mental image, but it's not a pleasant one. The fact that Karen's voice is there completely saves this song.

MCDANIEL: That's about a B-minus ballad in Songwriting 101 class.

SCHMIDT: Let's discuss "For All We Know," which was the lead single for this album.

MCDANIEL: Two of the guys from Bread wrote the song, but under pseudonyms. There are two things I've always loved about this song. Joe Osborn, the bassist, has a great lick at the beginning of the song. That beautiful upper-register bass playing became his hallmark. And there's an oboe duet. This is one of the only pop songs to ever have an oboe duet. Jim Horn and Bob Messenger were doublers on all those instruments, meaning they could play several different instruments like pit players in an orchestra. These were unusual instruments for a pop album.

WALLACE: This is a definitive Carpenters song and in the perfect key for Karen's voice. Everything about it is impeccable and the whole thing resonates with me and draws me in. It's incredibly well done. Just stunning.

JORDAN: This song defines them. It's the perfect Carpenters song, both vocally and instrumentally.

SCHMIDT: "Superstar" is such an atmospheric and moody song with a haunting melody. It had been recorded by Rita Coolidge on Joe Cocker's *Mad Dogs and Englishmen* album, but Richard first heard it sung by Bette Midler as a torch song on *The Tonight Show*.

MCDANIEL: My first exposure to this song was this beautiful arrangement. After that, no other renditions of it ever came close, including Leon Russell, who cowrote the song. He could never have imagined the magic that was going to happen when Karen got ahold of this vocal and Richard did that incredible arrangement. It may be his best.

SCHMIDT: We follow a groupie song with somewhat of a response

REVIEWS

"The LP is filled with changes-of-pace, resulting in a beautiful balance by the brother-sister team. Richard is the often-sought, rarely-found musical triple-threat man. In addition to vocalizing, he plays keyboards and arranged and orchestrated the songs. Come to think of it, he's actually a four-talent performer, for he also penned (with John Bettis) three of the vinyl's 10 tunes."
—Sherwood L. Weingarten, *Audio*

"Richard's sophisticated, contemporary arrangements and Karen's sparkling voice are the essence of the Carpenters' great success. These trademarks abound in their 3rd LP."
—*Billboard*

"The Carpenters have more going for them than against. There is no question that they have contributed mightily to the inherently limited genre of MOR music, that they bring a little light soul and sensitivity to a music that is by definition (almost) emotionally dehydrated. They have a WASPish charm that is pleasant to admire from a distance. And they do make fine singles. Period."
—Jon Landau, *Rolling Stone*

"Karen Carpenter's voice is pleasant, with a hint of an edge to it; Richard Carpenter's keyboards have the same quality; his and Karen's overdubbed back-up vocals fairly shimmer at times; the arrangements are clean, even tasteful. So why am I not happy? Probably because all these elements plus the kind of songs the Carpenters perform add up to schmaltz."
—*Stereo Review*

REFLECTIONS

We've always been "Carpenters." The idea is that we didn't want to sound like all the other groups—The Four Freshmen, The Beach Boys, The Diamonds, and the rest. So we just started calling ourselves "Carpenters."
—**Richard (1972)**

The Osmond Brothers have started calling themselves "Osmonds," the Lettermen have started calling themselves "Lettermen," and the Small Faces are calling themselves "Faces." And everybody's asking us why we changed our name from "The Carpenters." We've never been "The Carpenters."
—**Karen (1972)**

We had to change that one line, or "Superstar" wouldn't have been a hit. "Hardly wait to sleep with you again," which I think she put in just for shock value. I changed it to "be" with you. It never would have gotten to the top 40 otherwise. Now you can get away with "made love in my Chevy van," and Paul Simon can get away with "making love with Cecilia up in my bedroom," but he couldn't get away with "crap I learned in high school." They made Lou Christie recut "Rhapsody in the Rain" because he said, "making love in the rain." And "in this car love went much too far" had to be changed to "love came like a falling star." It still got the point across.
—**Richard (1975)**

I played the drums for three years and we were well into our third or fourth gold record before I got out front. At that point I was petrified because I didn't know what to do. My mouth still worked, but I didn't know what to do with my hands. I didn't know whether to walk or stand still or sit down or what the heck to do. Before, everything was working, and it was a cinch to play and sing and have a good time. But when I got out there, until I got comfortable with that, I just kind of planted myself and didn't really do anything. Now he has to tell me to stand still! I'm all over the place now.
—**Karen (1981)**

"Superstar," that's one of my favorites. Even though it wasn't tailor-made for Karen, it might as well have been tailor-made for Karen. It's a perfect song for her. It's a great melody and an off-beat lyric, but very touching and it worked well for my arrangemental skills. I just really like "Superstar." And that's one of few that for some reason Karen didn't seem to like all that much. Of course, she changed her mind.
—**Richard (1993)**

"Rainy Days and Mondays" is the greatest record I've heard of one of my songs. From the harmonica intro to the last notes it just made me crazy. When Karen sang it, you heard the sadness and the loneliness. For me, listening to her sing that song is almost like a bridge from what was contemporary to the roots of the emotion, back to a Billie Holiday kind of thing. It's just a classic.
—**Paul Williams (2002)**

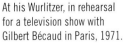

to groupies, **"Druscilla Penny," which is another Richard lead. That harpsichord solo is my favorite part.**

WALLACE: Don't even let me get started with "Druscilla." I have nothing good to say about it. If I had to pick one song that they absolutely should have left off the record, it's this song.

MCDANIEL: This is one of the most exposed moments for Richard, as far as his playing. It's the most unusual arrangement on the album, very strange, and with a gothic feel. There's a bass drum kick in an odd place on what would be the bridge of the song. When I got my LP, I was sure that mine had a scratch on it. But it turns out it was just a strange kick that didn't make any sense in the arrangement. It was intended, obviously, but I just have no idea why.

JORDAN: If I had a choice between "Saturday" and "Druscilla Penny," I'd keep "Druscilla Penny" and drop "Saturday." Or drop both songs for more Karen. I was resentful that it wasn't Karen's voice on those songs. Richard is half of the group and needed the attention, I suppose, but I just missed her voice.

MCDANIEL: I would love to have heard Karen sing "Saturday" the way Karen sang "Goofus." She had a good sense of humor for singing those novelty songs.

At his Wurlitzer, in rehearsal for a television show with Gilbert Bécaud in Paris, 1971.

With Ed Sullivan after receiving the Musical Group of the Year award from the American Guild of Variety Artists, December 1971.

SCHMIDT: "One Love" is next. It's another ballad by Richard and John Bettis and one that I assumed was probably a hit song when I first listened to the record.

MCDANIEL: It has a nice sense of flow and it's got a melodic line that really shows off Karen's voice. It's a mostly successful song, albeit one that ends with that aforementioned "happy chord."

WALLACE: It's a functional Carpenters song, but not exceptional.

SCHMIDT: The fast and furious "Bacharach/David Medley" is next. They were performing a version of this in concert, but it kicked off with "Any Day Now" and "Baby It's You." Even though this version is somewhat truncated, it's perfect in so many ways. Would you agree?

MCDANIEL: Yes. It's got the energy of a stage performance, which is reminiscent of that energy you hear in their early crude recordings from the late 1960s, some of which were released on the *From the Top* box set in 1991. It's a very well put together medley that allows them to indulge in all those overdubbed chords they loved so much. That's appropriate for these songs. The instrumentation is simple, with just Richard's Wurlitzer piano, bass, and drums. And the occasional English horn. I bought a Wurlitzer piano, simply because Richard played one. When he switched to Fender Rhodes around the time of the *Horizon* album, I sold my Wurlitzer and bought a Fender Rhodes. I wanted to be just like Richard!

WALLACE: I love this medley. My dad had reel-to-reels of a bunch of the original songs, like "Walk on By," "I'll Never Fall in Love Again," and "Do You Know the

Way to San Jose," so I was very familiar with these songs, and it was a thrill to hear the Carpenters do them. It's one of the brightest moments on this record.

MCDANIEL: Richard was a fine jazz pianist who rarely got to show it. I can count on one hand the number of times he got to play what I would call a jazz piano solo. This medley was one of the major ones, in the middle of "There's Always Something There to Remind Me." There was also a short acoustic piano solo in "This Masquerade" on *Now & Then*. We know from some of those early Richard Carpenter Trio recordings that he was quite capable as a jazz pianist, but he just didn't get to do it with their pop stuff all that often.

JORDAN: This is the one track where Richard Carpenter is the absolute star. Not vocally, but the arrangements are so incredible and so well put together. He's united these songs in such a way that it could have been a single. It shows off his fine abilities as an arranger.

SCHMIDT: We come now to "Sometimes," which closes out *The Tan Album* in such a simple and sophisticated way. Just the two of them doing what they do best.

JORDAN: A friend of mine, Sally Stevens, worked with Henry Mancini for years and did the demo on "Sometimes." I've heard her version and Richard and Karen didn't change a thing. It's just a simple piano and vocal. That's it.

MCDANIEL: This song showcases what makes the two of them special in one cut. It's just Richard being an artist and Karen being an artist, unadorned by anything else. And in typical Henry Mancini fashion, the last six bars or so is where all the magic happens. When my students are planning their musical theatre recitals, this would be what we call the "heartfelt encore." They end big, then have an intimate song that's just between them and the audience. That's what "Sometimes" is on this album. After the bustle of the "Bacharach/ David Medley," we have Karen and nothing else to distract from the beauty of her presenting these words. And she did so with as much honesty as any pop singer has ever been able to muster.

Inspecting their Grammys for Best Contemporary Vocal Performance by a Duo, March 1972.

4 A SONG FOR YOU

Released June 13, 1972
Produced by Jack Daugherty
Recorded at A&M Studios, Hollywood, CA

Top Billboard Position: #4

RIAA Certification: 3x Multiplatinum

Singles:
"Hurting Each Other" / "Maybe It's You"
"It's Going to Take Some Time" / "Flat Baroque"
"Goodbye to Love" / "Crystal Lullaby"
"Top of the World" / "Heather"
"I Won't Last a Day Without You" / "One Love"

with Harriet, Drew Jansen, and Joel Samberg

A SONG FOR YOU

The fourth Carpenters album marked the pinnacle of the duo's recording career with six songs that went on to become hit singles. Arranging "Goodbye to Love," Richard imagined the unlikely addition of a melodic fuzz guitar solo. They reached out to Tony Peluso, a guitarist for Instant Joy, the band that backed Mark Lindsay when he opened for several Carpenters concerts. The collaboration was instant simpatico.

Karen and Richard soon invited Peluso to join their road group. With the Carpenters entourage numbering fourteen, they began traveling on two Learjets, aptly named *Carpenter 1* and *Carpenter 2*. On a flight between one-nighters, John Bettis looked out the window and exclaimed, "Are we on top of the world now or what!" From that came "Top of the World," which they recorded for their *A Song for You* album, released in the summer of 1972.

In addition to "Goodbye to Love" and "Top of the World," *A Song for You* produced four more hit singles: "Hurting Each Other," "It's

A Song For You

(previous page)
Holding a promotional balloon for *A Song for You* at a party in their honor following their opening night at the Greek Theatre in Los Angeles, August 9, 1972.

Going to Take Some Time," "I Won't Last a Day Without You," and "Bless the Beasts and Children." The latter was previously released as a double A-side single with "Superstar" and was nominated for an Academy Award.

This was the last Carpenters album to bear a production credit for Jack Daugherty, who had helped get their demo tape to Herb Alpert back in 1969. Despite his billing as producer (which dated back to *Offering*), he was more of a contractor. Those were Richard's arrangements and productions. The duo's loyalty waned until the association ended abruptly after Richard read a *Cashbox* review praising Daugherty's production ability on *A Song for You*.

SCHMIDT: Some of Karen's best recordings were of songs by Leon Russell. The title song has gone on to become a modern pop standard, recorded by hundreds of singers, but the Carpenters version seems to be the definitive. What is it that makes this song so appealing?

HARRIET: "A Song for You" is my favorite song of all time. And Karen and Richard must have felt something very special about this song to name the record after it and have it as the opening and closing song. It's so touching and very powerful. It's what this album is all about for me. I love all the songs, but the title track is gold.

SAMBERG: It is this track in particular that makes me want to put the album at the top of my list. The album itself has quite a mix of styles. There's an abundance of intriguing orchestrations, the classic Carpenters multitrack vocals, and a very confident Karen using all the power and all the tools that she had. And this track uses it all.

JANSEN: She hits that D right near the beginning of the song. That's just where her money was, way down in the basement. Richard pitched that arrangement in that key to put her right down there in that note and it sends shivers up your spine.

(right)
Richard, late 1971.

HARRIET: Leon Russell's original performance is typical Leon Russell. You get all the emotion, but you can't quite make out the melody. Other versions were more like sketches, but Karen took the song and went over those pencil drawings with a clear, black ink pen and carefully painted the image exactly as it should look.

SAMBERG: By virtue of the theme and lyric, she's singing directly to us. The listener. It's one to one, like she's singing only to you. Also, the story is told from the perspective of somebody who has been around awhile. Somebody who has already seen it all, felt it all, had it all, loved it all and lost it all. Karen was only twenty-two when this album was released, but she sang it with such authority that you'd think she was a blues singer who had been around for fifty years.

HARRIET: When you're a young woman at that age, it's as if the world is coming to an end if your boyfriend dumps you. Whatever tiny thing has happened to you in life feels enormous and it's so easy to think that your whole life is terrible. But it's as if she made it OK to feel that way, even if you hadn't lived fifty years. She had the incredible gift of being able to communicate a sense of experience and wisdom through her vocals, even though she was so young.

JANSEN: When a new Carpenters album was released, my sister and I loved picking out the vocal lines in those wonderfully glorious passages, like the one right before the end of the bridge. "My love is in there hiding." They do that wonderfully quintessential Carpenteresque break and it's just a little moment of magic. There are quite a few on this album.

On tour, early 1972.

HARRIET: It feels to me like they sprinkled a little bit of Christmas on everything. Suddenly there's snow outside. It's all so magical.

SAMBERG: And what makes those magic moments especially effective, particularly in this song, is that they're not overdone. Despite Richard's prodigious skill as a composer and an arranger, he sometimes tended to overdo it. And why overdo it when your partner is Karen Carpenter? She doesn't need anything else.

SCHMIDT: "Top of the World" was a sleeper hit for the Carpenters, to say the least. The public had to beg for it to be released as a single.

SAMBERG: If you really wanted to pick this song apart, you might decide it's not that weighty. It's not that big of a deal. Yet it's mesmerizing. It's hard to find a misplaced note, vowel, or inflection. It's almost vocal perfection. And it's uplifting. Hearing her sing something so happy makes us feel good for her.

JANSEN: The second time you heard "Top of the World" you could sing along with it. And that was important. It's got that funny bass note on "looking *down*" near the end. When you were driving in the car and it came on the radio, everyone tried to outdo each other on that low note. It's just has all these little filigrees, including that lick on the Wurlitzer in the intro. That's a bear to play correctly and hardly anybody does it.

HARRIET: It's so uncanny and recognizable. There are so many little musical hooks that you find yourself singing along to. Not only to Karen's vocal, but the Wurlitzer piano part, the drums, and everything else.

SCHMIDT: "Hurting Each Other" has an almost Phil Spector "wall of sound" quality to it. This must have sounded amazing on the radio in 1972.

Afternoon sound check at the Muny amphitheatre, St. Louis, Missouri, July 10, 1972.

JANSEN: It did!

SAMBERG: Absolutely! It was the quintessential beach song for AM radio that year. I remember being at Jones Beach on Long Island and "Hurting Each Other" was the perfect song for it. It has such a singable hook and that harmony during the "gotta stop" phrase at the end is simply amazing.

HARRIET: In that first chorus, it's just her vocal, doubled. I love how they wait to bring in all the harmonies. First, it's two Karens, one in each ear, and then on the next chorus there are tons of her. All those signature layers emerge.

SCHMIDT: Another by-chance find was "It's Going to Take Some Time This Time." Richard first heard it on Carole King's *Music* LP when the engineers installing his new quadraphonic sound system used it to test the settings.

HARRIET: This song is a guilty pleasure. I used to sing in a jazz band when I was in my teens and we always put it in the set. Everyone loved this song. You could hear people singing along in the audience. You can't help but like it!

SAMBERG: It's the definition of sophisticated easy listening.

SCHMIDT: "Goodbye to Love" proved to be one of the duo's biggest hits of those penned by Richard and John Bettis.

SAMBERG: I will probably be the odd man out, so I'll just get it out of the way. I like it the least of all the cuts on the album. It's heavy, much like a metronome, and there are almost no breaks. Karen rarely gets to take a breath because of the way it's written.

JANSEN: It almost works better as an instrumental. It's more of a piano piece than a vocal piece. It leaves no room for breathing, but somehow Karen makes it through that whole damn line. It's one of my favorite songs and I like so many things about it.

On stage during a sold-out run at the Greek Theatre, August 1972.

HARRIET: I love this song, but I feel that the lyric is so unbelievably heartbreaking. The idea that somebody is just accepting loneliness as the answer to their life is so very sad. I love the guitar solo in it. It's one of their cooler records. Everything had been so clean-cut up to that point, so this dramatic guitar solo was quite groundbreaking. It's aggressive and daring.

JANSEN: It drew attention because it was so out of character for them. There are those stories of them receiving hate mail from fans who thought they'd sold out and gone acid rock!

SCHMIDT: Their sense of humor surfaces on "Intermission," the song that closes out side one. There weren't many pop groups in 1972 recording the music of Antonio Lotti.

HARRIET: Being English, I always found this hilarious, especially their pronunciation of the word bathroom as "bahthroom." It's funny and I love that about them. It appears Richard intended for this to be a concept album, so putting "Intermission" in the middle really fits with that idea.

JANSEN: If you consider side one to be act one, it leaves us in an up place, rather than down, after the dismal images of "Goodbye to Love."

SCHMIDT: "Bless the Beasts and Children" was tracked back in early 1971 during the *Tan Album* sessions and was the flipside for "Superstar." Is anyone familiar with the Stanley Kramer film?

JANSEN: I saw it shortly after it came out, but I couldn't tell you anything about it, other than the fact that there was a Carpenters song in it!

HARRIET: It's a beautiful arrangement and production. It ticks all the Carpenters boxes. But it doesn't quite give me the same feeling that so many other songs on this record do.

SAMBERG: It seems to lack the passion that most other Carpenters songs have.

SCHMIDT: "Flat Baroque" dates to the days of the Richard Carpenter Trio and their short-lived contract with RCA-Victor. This and "Piano Picker" are like a two-piece set, shining some light on Richard's talents.

JANSEN: I've always loved these two tracks back to back and agree they're cut from the same cloth. I was eleven when this came out, but I was already playing piano around town. It captivated me to know there was a song about playing the piano. I'd never heard one before.

REVIEWS

"Here's a super LP which will be another top seller for the Carpenters. Superb Jack Daugherty production and musicianship showcase the fine talent on such tunes as 'I Won't Last a Day Without You' (by Paul Williams) and 'Crystal Lullaby' (both by Richard Carpenter and John Bettis). Includes 'Hurting Each Other' and 'It's Going to Take Some Time.' Also dynamite readings of the title tune and of 'Goodbye to Love.'"
—**Billboard**

"The new Carpenters. Where to begin? The cover, maybe. It's a beautiful deep red—almost hypnotizing. Moving along to the record inside, we have nothing to offer but praise. Opening with Leon Russell's masterwork, 'A Song for You,' Karen and Richard offer warm and irrefutable proof that in their particular field they have no equals. . . . Watch this album rocket into the Top 10."
—**Cashbox**

"Karen's singing . . . grows more assured with each album. She is especially strong in her lower register, and she shows the potential of developing into an interesting stylist. . . . The title cut, Leon Russell's 'A Song for You' is far and away the album's finest moment. It is a great song that is rapidly achieving the classic status it deserves, and Karen communicates its poignancy with effortless serenity. . . . But above all, they will need to be more discriminating in their selection of material. Karen is capable of giving us considerably more than tiny sugar valentines."
—**Stephen Holden, *Rolling Stone***

"This new album . . . brings into sharp relief why the Carpenters are the most successful brother-sister team in show business since Fred and Adele Astaire. Professionalism and communication are the keys. They are absolutely professional without being cold. They communicate with each other and to the listener. *A Song for You* is a bright, extremely well-done album."
—***Stereo Review***

REFLECTIONS

The Song for You *cover. Whew . . . it's hard to explain. They came up with this heart, against a big red background. I said, "It's gonna look like a Valentine's Day card." "Oh no, you're wrong," they said, "this is hip, it's, it's camp. People will look at this and they'll say, oh yeah it's the Carpenters all right, but they're putting us on." I said, "They're gonna think it's a Valentine's Day card." I mean, that's what it looks like: a bunch of syrupy love songs, all packaged up with a heart on the front. On top of that, they put these stickers with a picture of the two of us, cheek to cheek, smiling . . . in the heart! It looked so . . . sweet! So . . . lovey dovey!*
—**Richard (1974)**

If you want to make money off a record, you should make it off an album. Not a single, save them for promotional things. Never think about royalties and money coming from a single. Even though we sell quite a few. To me, it's to help the album. The Song for You *album did two million and* Close to You *did more like four. If "Top of the World" had come out instead of "It's Going to Take Some Time," the* Song for You *album would have done another million units.*
—**Richard (1974)**

We were at home, getting ready to go on our European promotional tour in the Fall of '71. I was watching a Bing Crosby musical, Rhythm on the River. *In it he played a ghostwriter for a well-known songwriter, played by*

Basil Rathbone, who had lost his ability. In the plot, the character's best known song was called "Goodbye to Love." Now there was never a song called that in the movie, but good title! I heard the opening melody and came up with the first set of lyrics, but then my lyrics stopped. The music kept going to a point and then I wrote the rest of it when we were in Europe, in Berlin. And then I heard a big thing at the end, which eventually became the choral part with the guitar solo. That was written when I got back home. I called Bettis and said, "I got the song. It's called 'Goodbye to Love,' here's the first line, now finish it, please." And he did.
—**Richard (1986)**

"Goodbye to Love" caused a bit of controversy, due to the fuzz guitar solo. It's an accepted bit now in a power ballad to have a fuzz guitar, but back then it was a bit different and we did get some letters from dyed-in-the-wool fans who thought we'd sold out.
—**Richard (1994)**

Thanks to the Carpenters, A&M really had money. They didn't have money to burn but money to do things right. They treated people nicely. It was like the crème de la crème of the record companies at that time and a great place to be. There was a great creative energy to the lot.
—**Roger Nichols, composer (2002)**

Performing "Top of the World" during their first appearance on *The Bob Hope Special*, which aired October 5, 1972.

HARRIET: Even though they were a duo, Karen was usually in the spotlight. These two songs were a few minutes where it was able to be all about Richard.

SCHMIDT: "I Won't Last a Day Without You" was another underestimated song, which didn't see release as a single until 1974. It appears A&M couldn't imagine that one album could possibly generate so many hit singles.

JANSEN: This wasn't long after Carole King's *Tapestry*, which was one of those albums where everybody knew every song and it might as well have been her "greatest hits" album.

HARRIET: I love Paul Williams so much and think that the vision Richard had for his songs was incredible. It's almost anthemic. You can imagine it being sung in an arena with everybody singing along on the chorus.

JANSEN: I've always liked the Nichols and Williams stuff that they did, but I was kind of surprised that this one was released as a single.

SCHMIDT: "Crystal Lullaby" is an unusual song that dates to their college days and the vocal group Spectrum.

SAMBERG: It's a very early John Bettis lyric and sounds like a musicalization of prose. The vocals are great, the arrangement and instrumentation are fine, but there's no compulsion to hear it again and again.

JANSEN: I love what they do vocally. It's got that nice shimmer, the English horn, and it fades into "Road Ode" with the tinkling noises, but I always thought the imagery was too precious.

HARRIET: Karen's vocals are already so pure and caramelized. They just don't need all the extra sugar added on "Crystal Lullaby." It's easy to get a little distracted by all the sweetness and all the things going on around her voice.

SCHMIDT: "Road Ode," my favorite of all their album cuts, was written by band members Gary Sims and Dan Woodhams in 1971. Was this autobiographical for Karen and Richard?

JANSEN: This album was the apex. They were on the road 200 to 250 nights a year, which must have been horrible. The reality comes through in her performance. There's something almost angry about the arrangement of this song. The vocals are much more strident, and the backing vocals have much more of an edge to them. Bob

Messenger's flute solo at the end just blows me away. This is probably my favorite cut on the entire disc.

HARRIET: It's heavier. Karen is really belting here. It's not that beautifully airy sound we are used to, instead it's grittier and heavier, which is different for them.

JANSEN: The artwork on the inner sleeve of the LP had all these sweet little drawings that had something to do with some of the songs. Positioned next to the lyric for "Road Ode" was a road sign with a curved arrow pointing down. If the lyric didn't get you, the illustration sure would.

SAMBERG: This song is full of the *O* words that Karen had an affinity for. Words like go, home, load, road, and so on. As a song, it's mesmerizing. As a recording, it's mesmerizing. But as a message, it's an enigma to me. We all know how serious Richard was about the value of touring in the early days, but here it seems as if they are admitting to their fans that they hated doing it.

HARRIET: She doesn't do it with every delivery when she uses those same words in other songs. It varies depending on the time or album. It's quite endearing. She pronounced things so perfectly in every way, so when she sings certain words differently like that it makes your ears perk up.

SCHMIDT: The song "A Song for You" bookends this album and its haunting reprise brings the album to a close. Given Karen's story, hearing her sing the words "And when my life is over, remember when we were together" in 1972 probably had nowhere near the impact it does today.

SAMBERG: Richard knew exactly what he was doing by putting that on there, as if to say, "Hey folks, I have a sister here with an amazing voice that mesmerizes you, so stay tuned for our next album."

HARRIET: It's particularly interesting how it fades in. There is distance at first and she sounds very far away. Then she comes up close. For the closing of a song or a record, that is the reverse of what you would expect. On paper, you would think she would fade away or disappear, but she doesn't. She comes into vision. It's haunting. The reprise is very visual for me. I see her standing center stage, alone, and in a spotlight with some beautiful red velvet curtains behind her and an auditorium full of people, all completely silent. And then the light goes out. There's something powerful about "we were alone." And it is perhaps even more powerful now that she's gone.

Backstage before an Osmonds concert, 1972.

NOW & THEN

Released May 1, 1973
Produced by Richard and Karen Carpenter
Recorded at A&M Studios, Hollywood, CA

Top Billboard Position: #2

RIAA Certification: 2x Multiplatinum

Singles:
"Sing" / "Druscilla Penny"
"Yesterday Once More" / "Road Ode"

with Tom Smucker, Dena Tauriello, and Gary Theroux

During their 1972 summer tour, the Carpenters introduced a medley of "oldies-but-goodies," songs from the 1950s and 1960s that were enjoying a renaissance. The medley was so well received that they dedicated side two of their next album to it. Bookended with "Yesterday Once More," an ode to the oldies written by Richard and John Bettis, the songs were tied together like a radio show with the deejay ramblings of Tony Peluso.

The release of *Now & Then* on May 1, 1973, coincided with the Carpenters' performance for a state dinner honoring West German chancellor Willy Brandt at the White House in Washington, DC. Against the backdrop of the Watergate scandal, President Richard M. Nixon declared the Carpenters to be "young America at its very best." On drums was former Mickey Mouse Club Mouseketeer Cubby O'Brien, who had recently joined the road group.

The *Now & Then* LP was presented in a striking double gatefold jacket featuring a panoramic artistic rendering of the siblings driving

(previous page)
Photo session outtake, 1973.

in Richard's red 1972 Ferrari past their huge Downey home. The residence had recently undergone an extensive remodel and expansion including a billiards room, wine cellar, and state-of-the-art soundproof music room. In back was a Japanese garden with artificial waterfalls and streams, adorned with wooden bridges and various ornaments of the Orient.

Commonly referred to as the "Now & Then House," the dwelling at 9828 Newville Avenue became a Graceland-style destination for Carpenters fans. The senior Carpenters lived there until Harold's death in 1988 and Agnes's in 1996, but the property sold in 1997 and fell into disrepair. A large portion was leveled to make way for an oversized McMansion, but the main portion of the house has eluded the wrecking ball.

SCHMIDT: The Carpenters recorded several concept albums, but this one may be the most distinctive in terms of arrangement and presentation. Let's jump right in and discuss "Sing," which opens the album and was the first single.

THEROUX: "Sing" originated as one of many original tunes written by Joe Raposo for *Sesame Street*. The idea of an adult pop group covering material from *Sesame Street* might seem a little surprising, but Karen really loved the song. They decided to give it a shot and it turned out to be the lead track and one of their biggest hits.

SMUCKER: It didn't seem like a song from *Sesame Street* should work, but it really worked, and it was a big hit. That says something about the Carpenters, their skillset, and their risk taking. It wasn't like any other pop groups wanted to cover something from

"Young America at its very best." With West German Chancellor Willy Brandt, President Richard Nixon, and First Lady Pat Nixon in the East Room at the White House, May 1, 1973.

Sesame Street. It's a great way for this album to begin. It's got that Carpenters magic in terms of the vocal and production.

TAURIELLO: It's a perfect illustration of the Carpenters magic. By most people's ideology or standards, it was a song that had no right to be a hit. They do what they do and all of a sudden, it's a smash. It was a nontraditional approach to a pop song, for sure.

SCHMIDT: In stark contrast to "Sing" was "This Masquerade," which was one of the duo's most sophisticated arrangements and recordings. Part of it is due to Richard's lengthy, jazz-influenced piano solo, but the thing that stands out to me most is Karen's drumming.

TAURIELLO: One of the reasons I wanted to talk about this record is that she drummed on virtually all of it. The material on *Now & Then* is just straight-up pop tunes, but one of the many reasons I love her drumming is that she plays for the song. "This Masquerade" is a great example. It's such a brilliantly simple and sophisticated part. It comes from the idea of what they call the "Ray Price Shuffle," which is a brush in one hand and a backbeat with the left hand. It's so elegantly simple and perfect for the tune and I love it. It's so brilliant.

THEROUX: It's interesting that millions of people fell in love with Karen's voice, but so few of them knew she was a reluctant vocalist. She considered herself primarily to be a drummer. And she was perfectly happy to hide behind the drum kit and not even show her face in concert, but that voice was just so incredible.

SCHMIDT: Dena, would you please share the story about the time you met Karen when you were just a little girl?

TAURIELLO: My obsession with them came at a very early age and I met them when I was seven. I was already aware that she was a drummer and I was into all their music. When they played the Westchester Premier Theater in New York, my parents arranged for us to go back during the intermission, following their opening act of Skiles and Henderson. I nearly passed out when Karen opened the door. She had a giant smile and was the loveliest person. I remember her warmth and her kindness. We went back out and I watched her drum during the show. I remember walking away saying, "That's amazing. That's what I want to do." And I started taking lessons when I was eight years old.

SMUCKER: It was the incredible cover that got me interested in this album. I was living in New York City and there was an ad for *Now & Then* on the subway. It was just this incredible cover stretched out. To me it's the greatest Carpenters album cover. I was struck by the fact that it was just them driving down the street in that red Ferrari. There's also something about it that's striking and powerful. Seeing the cover over and over again on the subway made me go out and buy this record.

SCHMIDT: Tom, you wrote an entertaining piece for the *Village Voice* back in 1975 that focused the duo's image and the stigma that came with buying a Carpenters record. You said: "I rehearsed how and where I would attempt my Carpenters' record purchase. Trying to overcome my worst case of consumer stage fright since I first bought rubbers years ago. What would the man behind the counter say when I walked up with my Carpenters record?" That's priceless! Were you really that guy in the record store?

SMUCKER: That spoke to something that was real. The Carpenters were incredibly popular at the time, but also out of fashion. Karen Carpenter had that unique voice that rivaled Linda Ronstadt and others around at that time, and Richard Carpenter was an amazing composer and producer, but there was something about their image or their presentation. They were certainly considered square.

THEROUX: Recording a song like "Sing" didn't help it. The important thing to consider, though, is who you want to please. What is your target demo? Do you want to please the self-appointed "experts" at *Rolling Stone* or do you want to please America? Fortunately, Richard and Karen were smart enough to realize that the only critics that counted were the ones who

were going to be requesting their music on the radio and buying their records. The sales underscore that.

SMUCKER: Pop music was becoming aware of itself in a certain way it hadn't been in the late 1950s and early 1960s. The good review and the bad review were a part of that machinery as well.

THEROUX: It's constantly evolving. For me, there are certain producers, like Phil Spector, George Martin, Brian Wilson and a handful of others, who I put at the pantheon of producers. The records the Carpenters made rank right up there among the finest crafted recordings anybody has ever made. As I told them when I interviewed them. it doesn't matter what these critics say. The people who recognize quality know exactly what you are doing, and they appreciate it.

SCHMIDT: "Heather," the only instrumental on the album, originated as "Autumn Reverie" and was written as underscore for a Geritol TV commercial. Do you feel this was just filler or perhaps something more inspired?

SMUCKER: Maybe it was just thrown in as filler, but I like it. It fits the flow of the album. After all, "We've Only Just Begun" was originally a bank commercial.

THEROUX: It's a nice instrumental which creates a satisfying emotional bridge between the songs which precede and follow it. One of the first things you learn as a radio or album programmer is pacing via musical tempos, textures, and content.

TAURIELLO: I love the instrumentation. The bass, drums, and even the piano approach it like a pop tune, even though it's heavily orchestral and almost classical in its feel and presentation.

SCHMIDT: Let's discuss "Jambalaya." Carpenters cover Hank Williams. This was a huge hit in the UK but didn't see release as a single here in the States.

SMUCKER: It may have worked in England since it was one step removed, but I never really liked that cut. Perhaps I was too familiar with Hank Williams and country music. It's the one piece on

REVIEWS

"A unique concept—that of placing new versions of old tunes such as 'Johnny Angel' and 'Our Day Will Come' in the form of an old DJ radio show with DJ and everything sets this LP above other LPs. Some radio stations are playing that entire side as a separate radio 'show.' But the flip side is also jammed with hits and Karen Carpenter's charming voice, clear and melodious, virtually turns this LP into a classic. . . . This should be another million-seller for the duo."
—*Billboard*

"Side One's alright, just what you needed; more of that nice, syrupy, ultra commercial pap. 'Sing' is one of their all time best singles, and the essence of the act: 'Sing of good things not bad.' But Karen's reading of 'Jambalaya' is almost as bad as John Fogerty's, and there may be gray clouds passing over Carpenterland because she manages to sound almost used in Leon Russell's 'This Masquerade' while 'I Can't Make Music' is the Carpenters' hymn of despair like Traffic's 'Sometimes I Feel So Uninspired.'"
—**Lester Bangs**, *Let It Rock*

"To say the least, their renditions of such rock classics of 'Da Do Ron Ron,' 'Johnny Angel,' and 'Fun, Fun, Fun,' among others are letter perfect. . . . Karen and Richard have never sounded better and this album is truly destined for the gold mine."
—*Cashbox*

"What a record! Karen Carpenter has a voice in the great tradition of Judy Collins, Joan Baez, and other white middle-class women. Somehow expressive and full of allusion in its basic mournful/depressed impressiveness. Both presenting the surface of middle-class life and suggesting its deepest hidden feelings."
—**Tom Smucker**, *Village Voice*

REFLECTIONS

Richard had this dream about a vocal sound for a pop group and he said to me, "I've got this sister who sings and plays the drums." And I said, "No you don't!" So we started writing songs and we put the group together behind Richard's idea and his concept. Richard and I have always written fast and written easily. To write with Richard is to write with one of the most intelligent and aware people that I've ever met in the record business because he pays attention to what's going on. He's been listening to records avidly for 15 years and he loves the business he's in.
—**John Bettis, lyricist (1974)**

The cover for Now & Then. *That was supposed to be—very original—a picture of us standing in front of the house, smiling. I said, "No, no, no." Then it was, "Well, what else can we do now that we're here, how about if you get in your car and drive down the street." Immediately someone sees the picture of us in the car and says, "You're not smiling. You look mad." "No," I said, "I just don't smile when I drive. If I were smiling it would look like a 1952 DeSoto ad!"*
—**Richard (1974)**

In the whole nostalgia thing, we cut the Now & Then *album, but we never released anything other than "Yesterday Once More." One day, we were driving on the freeway and it was right in the middle of everybody releasing oldies. [Richard] said, "You know, nobody's ever written anything about the surge coming back." I could see the head lighting up right before we got off at Highland. That was it. Five minutes later, out came the tune.*
—**Karen (1976)**

There are a lot of things on the Now & Then *album that we wanted to release as singles, but we were afraid of getting stuck in an oldies thing. There is still one, though, that I want to do, and that's "Foolish Little Girl." Oh, it really rips me to shreds! I love it! And another one: "My Boyfriend's Back." Oh, there are a lot of them. I could go on for days. There are so many good ones.*
—**Karen (1978)**

President Nixon was a fan and he was going to be entertaining Chancellor Brandt from West Germany and the White House contacted management about the Carpenters being the musical entertainment for the evening. We were delighted! No matter who the President is, even if you didn't vote for him, he's still the President of the United States. And to be in the White House meeting the President of the United States? Absolutely!
—**Richard (1986)**

One reviewer, I'll never forget, was writing about [side one of] our album Now & Then, *which ended with a Randy Edelman tune called "I Can't Make Music." And this guy writes: "The album finishes with a song called 'I Can't Make Music,' to which, regarding the Carpenters, I can only add, 'Right on.'" And I'm thinking, wait a minute! You may not like the style of our music, but don't tell me we can't make music.*
—**Richard (1988)**

the album that just doesn't fit. If I were to pick a Hank Williams song for the Carpenters to work their magic on, it wouldn't have been this one.

SCHMIDT: I suppose it didn't really fit with the "Now" side of the album, being that it was first a hit in 1952, a full decade before most of the oldies on side two.

THEROUX: They were just having fun with the song, and they probably had a great time recording it. It was supposed to be something light. And it very possibly introduced a lot of pop people to Hank Williams.

TAURIELLO: As a five- or six-year-old, I really liked it. I didn't know anything about Hank Williams and had no exposure to the original, so I just thought it was a fun tune. I still enjoy it now, but it sticks out a little, like almost not belonging on that record.

Performing "Sing" in concert with a children's choir, 1973.

SCHMIDT: "I Can't Make Music" was a Randy Edelman tune, a song he played while opening for Karen and Richard on tour. It's long been one of my favorite Carpenters album tracks.

TAURIELLO: It might be my favorite on the record. It's a fabulous album cut. I have always loved that song. Love her vocal, love the arrangement.

SMUCKER: I agree. It's a perfect side-one closer. Sung by the wrong person or produced by the wrong person, that song would sound too sad. But Karen's vocals are so deep and there's a lot of stuff going on there.

THEROUX: There are some singers who will attack a song, vocally. They might as well be singing the phone book because they're not really paying attention to what the composer or lyricist had in mind. Clearly, Karen was not like that. Words meant an enormous amount to her. She was very careful to interpret these songs in a way that truly conveyed a feeling she felt people could identify with.

TAURIELLO: It doesn't at all feel intentional to me either. It's just who she was, instinctively. It was her tremendous ability as a vocalist. It wasn't intentional. It wasn't as if she gave it a lot of thought. It just came out of her.

THEROUX: I think that's largely true, but she *did* give a lot of thought to the lyrics. I remember when I interviewed Gladys Knight, she said, "I really am actually an actress. I'm acting to music. For three minutes I'm playing the brokenhearted and rejected lover. Right after that I'm upbeat and happy. Then right after that I'm in a different mood." One of the great things about Karen was that she was able to tackle so many kinds of emotions and convey them with such sincerity that you absolutely believed every single note.

On the beach at Pie de la Cuesta, Acapulco, Mexico, June 1973.

Warming up for a charity softball game, Sawtelle Field, Westwood, CA, August 8, 1973.

SCHMIDT: Let's flip to side two and talk about "Yesterday Once More," written by Richard and John Bettis. It proved to be their biggest worldwide hit and at one point was #1 in Belgium, England, Hong Kong, Israel, Japan, Malaysia, Singapore, and Venezuela.

SMUCKER: I feel it's really a deep song. You can listen through it quickly and it feels that it's nice to remember the old songs you've forgotten, they're back on the radio, and so on. But when I really listen to the song and look at the words, there are complications in it that make it a really deep kind of song. And that matches up with Karen's voice. In one way it's just a clear, beautiful voice, but in another way, it's a very deep voice with a lot of different emotions in it.

THEROUX: There was always a little hint of sadness in Karen's voice. This song talks about that sadness, but it combines it with an uplifting feeling. Combining those two emotions into one song is magical. There's an emotional dichotomy there, too.

SMUCKER: It doesn't go from being sad, to being happy. It's got both going on at the same time. Pretty interesting.

TAURIELLO: I always liked the song, but as I've gotten older I love it more and more. As you get older, you get further removed from songs that you grew up on. You hear those songs and you can immediately recall a memory, a smell, or where you were. You have a good feeling, hopefully, or a memory that goes along with that. You get all that from this song. And now, "Yesterday Once More" is one of those songs for me.

THEROUX: Part of the irony is that the Carpenters are now part of that "yesterday."

SCHMIDT: Let's move to the oldies medley that inhabits the rest of side two. They started doing the medley in some form as early as their 1972 summer tour. It has been revealed since then that putting this on the album was out of desperation. They needed an album but didn't have time to search for new material.

THEROUX: Karen and Richard loved the oldies. In Los Angeles, there were two big oldie stations, KRTH and KRLA. When I was programming for KRLA, all the songs in this medley were played in heavy rotation. I later learned that Karen and Richard were listening to that programming and it's out of that they developed this list of favorites that they built into this medley.

SMUCKER: As a Beach Boys fanatic, I'm going to complain about both "Fun, Fun, Fun" and Jan and Dean's "Deadman's Curve." I'm not the big fan

Modeling the official
Carpenters Fan Club T-shirts.

of Richard's singing. Although I know it's unfair, I always compare these to their originals, particularly for those two songs. I saw them do this medley live. When it's live, it works in a completely different way. As for "Johnny Angel," Karen really improves it. It's almost a different song and certainly a much deeper song.

THEROUX: "The Night Has a Thousand Eyes" was probably the best song Bobby Vee ever recorded. It was just a fun song and that's probably the reason why it's in there. "Our Day Will Come" was originally a hit for Ruby and the Romantics in 1963. The other track after that, "One Fine Day," is one of Karen's best performances. When I put the box set together for *Reader's Digest*, I said to Richard, "This track is so good that you really need to go back to the multitrack, duplicate what you have there, and add a bridge to make it a complete song." But he never did it.

SCHMIDT: Speaking of that box set, you somehow convinced Richard to let you break up the medley and present the songs without Tony Peluso's DJ narration in between. How did that come to be?

THEROUX: I was a DJ when the album came out, and I found Tony's interjections to be irritating. Maybe it was fun in concert, but it was annoying on record. When the box set came around, I told Richard I'd like to separate the tracks in the *Now & Then* medley so that we can hear the entire track from beginning to the end and without the DJ overdubs. I was quite surprised when he said, "Oh, OK." He went back into the multitrack, pulled the voice out, separated the tracks, and all the tracks from that medley, except for "Da Doo Ron Ron," wound up in the set.

SMUCKER: I want to give a shout out to the final reprise of "Yesterday Once More." I always felt that was a really great way of pulling it all together.

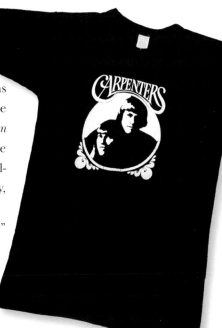

THE SINGLES
1969–1973

Released November 9, 1973
Produced by Richard and Karen Carpenter,
Jack Daugherty
Recorded at A&M Studios, Hollywood, CA

Top Billboard Position: #1

RIAA Certification: 7x Multiplatinum

with Justin Vivian Bond, Nath Ann Carrera,
Gina Garan, and Ted Ottaviano

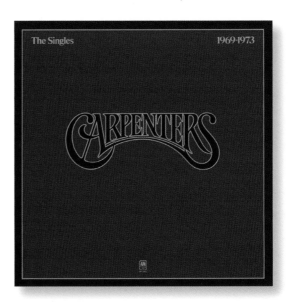

The year 1974 began with *The Singles 1969–1973* at the top of the *Billboard* album chart. This greatest hits collection contained nine million-sellers and was their first and only #1 album in the United States. Sales eventually topped twelve million units in the United States alone, and it remained at the top of the United Kingdom album chart for a total of seventeen weeks. "Top of the World" became their second #1 single, providing the perfect promotional push for the LP.

There were 203 Carpenters concerts in 1974, with sold-out tours across Europe and Japan. Tickets to three weeks of their shows in Japan sold out in less than an hour and were enjoyed by some eighty-five thousand fans. The reception at Tokyo's airport was in true rock star fashion with mobs of screaming fans snapping pictures, pulling at their clothes, and rocking their limousine.

Back home in the United States, they played a week at New York's

Westbury Music Fair, two four-week stints at the Riviera in Las Vegas, and two weeks at the Sahara Tahoe. They also returned to the Hollywood Bowl for a sold-out performance for more than eighteen thousand and taped a live concert for television with Arthur Fiedler and the Boston Pops.

Although their greatest successes stemmed from their studio recordings, the Carpenters spent most of their professional time on tour. In 1971 they played upward of 150 shows. They did 174 concerts in both 1972 and 1973. Six weeks on the road doing one-nighters was not uncommon. Upon learning it would take a minimum of 150 shows a year to see any profit, they knew it was time to cut back.

Their demanding schedule had left little time to record new music, but three singles were issued in 1974: "I Won't Last a Day Without You" (by then two years old and the sixth single from *A Song for You*), "Santa Claus Is Comin' to Town" (a track leftover from a 1972 session), and one new recording, "Please Mr. Postman." A Motown hit for the Marvelettes, "Postman" became the Carpenters' third #1 single.

Taking a bow during their two-week run at the Riviera in Las Vegas, October 1974.

SCHMIDT: Because it's a compilation, this album wasn't originally on my list for inclusion in this book. Right away, though, several commentators demanded I reconsider. What is it about this collection that makes it so special?

OTTAVIANO: I love this record. It's got the ten commandments on it: in terms of the Carpenters sound, it's got all the definitive tracks together in one group. My family got it when I was little, and I remember thinking the cover was a fusion of the Partridge Family's first album cover and *Jesus Christ Superstar* put together. I was drawn to it then and I've grown to love it even more. They've done greatest hits and so many other compilations, but this one works in a way that the other ones don't for me. With the combination of songs here, I'm happy to say Richard hit a homer on this one.

GARAN: *The Singles* is a definitive album, loaded with pathos. There are so many cuts that I love on this album, but I consider it more of a beginner's album or a primer into the Carpenters. I prefer the stuff that no one ever listens to.

CARRERA: Karen is my favorite singer, and the Carpenters are my favorite duo. I immerse myself in them quite often. I agree with Gina. This is an album from an era that I love but not one I listen to often. When I encounter people who are not well versed in the Carpenters, I always steer them away from this album. I think of them as an album band. You can't really understand the Carpenters until you've heard side two of their first four albums. That's where you start getting into the more experimental time signatures, their anticapitalist numbers, and so on. I always steer people to conceptualize them as album artists versus singles artists.

BOND: I'm with you on that as well. When it comes to the albums, I really like most of the darker, sadder songs. When I was a kid, though, my father said, "Always buy the greatest hits albums. They have all the songs you want to hear." Once again, my father was wrong! I like the songs you don't hear on the radio. I was a kid when this record came out and I loved all the hit songs. But they weren't the songs that made me feel the things I wanted to feel when I listened to the Carpenters.

SCHMIDT: Vivian, I came across a piece on your recent Lincoln Center performance and there was a mention of "squares and misfits" who find solace in Carpenters recordings. What do you think it is about their music, and specifically Karen's voice, that draws us in and provides a sense of comfort?

BOND: When you're young, everybody wants you to always be happy. Someone pulls out the camera and says, "Smile!" And you must smile, whether you feel like it or not. I was always being forced to perform as the good child and be the boy my parents wanted me to be. But when I listened to Karen Carpenter sing, I could let that forced identity slip away. I could explore my own feelings and thoughts about who I was. Being a trans kid, there was something missing. But I felt that Karen Carpenter understood that. It seems like she was almost aware that *she* was not what she was supposed to be. For the geeks, misfits, and outsiders, we felt a recognition and intellectually grasped something that a lot of people listening to her songs probably didn't even think about.

SCHMIDT: Gina, you have a son named Carpenter. Is that just a coincidence?

GARAN: No, I wanted to name him (Karen) Carpenter, with the Karen in parentheses, but my ex-husband wouldn't let me. I said, "I will never call him Karen unless we're alone," but he wouldn't allow it. Carpenter and I are contemplating getting a dog and naming it Karen. Then when it's time for dinner I can scream, "Karen, Carpenter, time to eat!"

SCHMIDT: And you were involved in the making of the Todd Haynes cult classic *Superstar: The Karen Carpenter Story*. Tell me about your association with that film.

Relaxing at their Las Vegas hotel before a concert, late 1974.

Traveling with the band: Danny Woodhams, Tony Peluso, Bob Messenger, Cubby O'Brien, and Doug Strawn.

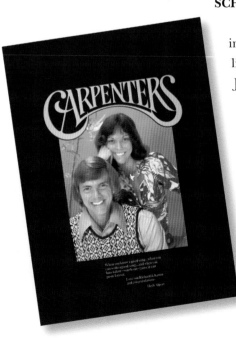

GARAN: I used to work at Boy Bar on Eighth Street and Todd Haynes was a customer there. I overheard him say something about Karen Carpenter and dolls. Those are the only two things I think about. Ever! I was curious to know what he was doing. We started chatting and I told him I had hundreds of dolls, so I lent him a lot of the dolls that were in the film. And he never gave them back!

SCHMIDT: Let's dig into the album now, beginning with the intro and overture.

OTTAVIANO: I thought it was so smart that they started the album with the intro of "Close to You" because it's so iconic and so identifiable. I just love these little segues, which Richard did on several of their albums. I always thought that Janet Jackson was doing a nod to the Carpenters with all her interludes on *The Velvet Rope*. But I love this album and I love the fact that Richard's constantly polishing these recordings. Both he and Karen had this OCD about them and they were always refining their craft.

CARRERA: I love that their albums have bookend songs, starting all the way back with *Offering* and that choral intro/outro. It gives them room to be a little bit more experimental at times, like at the end of *A Song for You*, and the reprise where she is coming out of that black hole of reverb. Then on *Horizon* there was "Aurora" and "Eventide." That is an essential part of the Carpenters album sound. I'm glad they are always paying attention to details like that. It certainly gave structure to their albums.

SCHMIDT: "Top of the World" first appeared on the *A Song for You* album in 1972. That version was simple and sparse. A nice album cut, but not all that radio-friendly.

OTTAVIANO: The original was definitely sparser. And they modified that steel guitar sound some to keep it from being labeled as a country song. The newer mix felt like it was ready for pop radio.

CARRERA: This is the one of the redone vocals of Karen's that I love. I love the *Song for You* cut, too, and think it's still an excellent vocal take, but her vocal sails the highs and lows effortlessly here. It's a joy to listen to with that souped-up '70s country guitar part and backing vocals. I prefer the *Singles* version to the original version.

BOND: It's sunnier. It was also their pathway to hokiness. This song seemed to lead them away from their serious, beautiful balladry and into their live show and that '70s hokey pop variety moment that went on way too long and, at the end of the day, kind of destroyed their legacy.

OTTAVIANO: There were some hokey songs on the early albums too, though.

BOND: But they weren't as ubiquitous.

OTTAVIANO: With "Top of the World," they couldn't beat it down with a club. It got so much attention as an album cut that they had to finally succumb and release it as a single.

CARRERA: The success of "Top of the World" is what led into "Please Mr. Postman," essentially.

With date Mike Curb at the 16th Annual Grammy Awards, Karen's 24th birthday, March 2, 1974.

Backstage at the Hollywood Palladium with Bette Midler after presenting her with the Grammy for Best New Artist, March 2, 1974.

GARAN: "Postman" was the hokiest video they ever did!

CARRERA: That's the sad Disneyland video with Richard looking pissed that he must be in the video and on a ride! I've watched hundreds of hours of Carpenters documentaries and TV time. When you see her on those TV shows, she seemed forced into that feminine look and appearance with the piled-on hair falls. And when she's not playing drums in those videos, she's still doing kick drums, drumming on herself, and tapping her feet. That's all she wanted to do, but it was gender subversive at that time for a girl to play drums. They pulled her off the drums because she was a threat to the status quo. It was uncomfortable seeing her brought out from behind the drums and being forced into the role of a lead singer.

SCHMIDT: Another song that underwent a huge makeover was "Ticket to Ride." Let's compare the original 1969 version with this redo.

OTTAVIANO: You can really hear that she found her sound between that first album in 1969 and this one in 1973. She must have felt that she needed to go back to that recording with her new and definitive sound. What's so cool about "Ticket to Ride" is that it's a Beatles song, of course, but it also had that special message during the outro. "Think I'm gonna be sad," just over and over again. They knew their messaging, whether it was conscious or not.

CARRERA: I highly prefer the original version of "Ticket to Ride," personally. I love their first few albums. Every line that Karen sang was like a dirge and rendered with such feeling. To me, this new version was stripped of all emotion. It's stylistically in touch with the rest of the album, but it's interesting that they called it *The Singles 1969–1973* and then just left off 1969. But I also love the snow video with her in the headband. It's stilted and amazing!

SCHMIDT: Next comes the holy trinity of Carpenters hits. The combo of these three songs worked well for them in concert for many years. Let's talk first about "Superstar," which is my favorite of all Carpenters songs. It's so atmospheric. No matter how many times I hear it, it still gives me chills.

BOND: That's the quintessential song for me. It's such a personal thing. I heard that song on the radio at a time when I didn't know yet how much I loved music or that I wanted to be a singer.

REVIEWS

"This greatest hits package affirms the act's fine talent. Karen's clear, clean, pristine tones have a glisten whether it's heard on 'We've Only Just Begun' or 'Top of the World.' Placed end-to-end, the group's music has a compelling quality which stands the test of time."
—*Billboard*

"Thinking about the perfect present to buy your dead grandmother? How about an album full of dead wood?"
—Ed Naha, *Circus*

"Not their 'greatest hits,' you understand. Just a modest, dignified album made up of the singles which, in four years, have boosted the Carpenters into the top flight of charts and popularity polls. Up-to-date, too. Includes 'Top of the World.' [. . .] A strong compilation album."
—Peter Jones, *Record World*

"Heard together, the duo's hits prove that Richard Carpenter didn't study music at Yale for nothing. His clean arrangements, delicate piano turns and conservatively employed strings enhance almost every cut, and after a few tracks it becomes obvious his contributions have been grossly underestimated."
—Paul Gambaccini, *Rolling Stone*

"Perhaps it's to cater to late-coming Carpenters fans that a new album is being released to coincide with their British tour. As might be expected, this contains 12 of their biggest hits, which together make a very attractive proposition for the record buyer. I'm unable to detect a weak spot in the choice of material. . . . The old adage about the only certain things in this world being birth, death and income tax can now be definitely rewritten—a fourth certainty has appeared, and that is the Carpenters' new album, and their European tour will be among the great successes of 1974. Actually, it's equally certain that I'll be there to watch."
—John Tobler, publication unknown

REFLECTIONS

I feel the term "greatest hits" is really an overused thing. Individuals and groups with two or three hits all of a sudden put them on one album, use filler for the rest, and title it "great." This album contains eleven true hits, yes, but it wasn't just slapped together. We've remixed a few, recut one and joined a couple of others. It's simply something I feel we owe to our audience and ourselves.
—Richard (1974)

How many people can you name—and I'm not on an ego trip, this is a fact—that have had hit singles, one right after another after another? It's a type of thing where it takes a certain talent to be able to pick something that becomes a hit single.
—Richard (1975)

John Bettis came out on one of our one-nighter excursions, just to hang out. We were chartering a couple of Learjets and he got the idea for a title called "Top of the World," as a result of being in the Lear. As soon as I heard the title, I heard the chorus. The tune kept going and the verse came afterwards, and I gave him a call. That turned out to be a much more popular song than I ever thought it would be. I thought it was a nice song and a nice album cut, but it turned out to be a worldwide smash.
—Richard (1986)

It was a phenomenon in Japan, definitely. "Close to You" did well, but the one that really broke through there was "Superstar." We went over very briefly for a promotional tour with one concert in '70. We went over for full tours in '72, '74, and '76. By '74, the song that went absolutely crazy there was "Yesterday Once More." With that, combined with "Top of the World" and the Now & Then *album, we became like the Beatles over there. When we went over in '74, it was not to be believed. It was like a mob scene at the airport!*
—Richard (1986)

Richard actually rerecorded that steel guitar part on "Top of the World" three separate times. He couldn't find anybody to play what he heard. He tried a guy named Red Rhodes, he tried another guy I can't remember, and then he finally got the number of Buddy Emmons, possibly the best steel player of the latter twentieth century in Nashville, Tennessee. Buddy Emmons was just an astonishing genius at steel. The other guys had struggled, and Buddy came in and Richard showed him what he wanted and he just kinda shrugged and went out and played it perfectly. But Richard's that guy. It was a steel part. Nobody but he would've known it wasn't perfect. But Richard rerecorded it three times until he got what he wanted.
—John Bettis (2014)

In concert before a sold-out crowd at the Hollywood Bowl, September 6, 1974.

Live in Japan album and poster from King Records in Japan, 1974.

I went home and it was in my head all night long and I even dreamed about it. I went to school the next day and got up for show-and-tell and told them that I had written a song. I was too nervous to sing in front of everyone, so I stood behind the TV and sang what I remembered of "Superstar" to the class. The teacher said, "Are you *sure* you wrote that song?" I told her, "Yes, I wrote it last night in bed." Later, I heard it on the radio and I was mortified that I had *not* written that song, as it turned out. That song was the Carpenters song that just broke my heart. And it still does.

SCHMIDT: Let's talk about "Rainy Days and Mondays."

GARAN: "Rainy Days" was my first song I can recall hearing and loving as a child. I will never forget it. I was in my parents' bedroom and they had a headboard with an eight-track tape deck and surround sound speakers built into it. I plugged in those earmuff headphones, laid back, and then "Rainy Days" came on. I remember looking out and it was raining. I thought the song was written for me. I was probably no more than five years old and I just remember feeling like I was in love with whoever was singing and feeling like I found my place in the world.

SCHMIDT: "Goodbye to Love" and its fuzz guitar solo proved to be more than some listeners could handle.

BOND: I just think it's sick that Richard wrote a song for his sister to sing that had such sad lyrics. It's no wonder she was depressed if she had to sing that every night in front of thousands of people! And that phrase has no breath in it whatsoever. It really throws down the gauntlet for every other singer. And it certainly isn't kind to people who want to cover that song and have smoked in their life!

CARRERA: I love the original mixes of "Rainy Days and Mondays" and "Goodbye to Love" before they were altered for this album. Richard sped up the recordings to try to match the key with "Superstar," at least on the vinyl version. Karen, being an alto, had this great, low, tomboy voice. But when

you speed up an alto voice, it sounds like a forced feminization of her voice. Pair that with her having already been ripped off the drums.

SCHMIDT: Ted, you developed and taught a class at the Rock and Roll Hall of Fame. It's unlikely that they'll ever induct the Carpenters, but soft rock is still rock, isn't it?

OTTAVIANO: My prayers were answered when ABBA got inducted into the Rock and Roll Hall of Fame. I couldn't see that happening. I do think the Carpenters deserve to be in there, but the Hall of Fame is such a straight white boys club. There really haven't been many surprises over the years. Lately, they seem to be starting to loosen up a bit, so never say never.

SCHMIDT: What would releasing "This Masquerade" instead of "Sing" have done for their reputation?

CARRERA: "This Masquerade" is one of my favorite Karen vocals and it would have been wise to release it. When you subject people to a children's choir, your music's going to take on a different sound.

BOND: I was a kid when "Sing" came out. I loved it because I felt like Karen totally understood me. She was my ideal of this cool teenage hippy girl. To me she was like the dream babysitter. The perspective I took on that song was that I was a kid, it was a pop song with kids in it, and it was sung by somebody who I thought was amazing.

SCHMIDT: Does anyone else feel that the celebration of these twelve hits in this practically perfect package was like a big middle finger to the critics who had called Carpenters music "saccharin" or "wallpaper music" and been so dismissive to their work?

OTTAVIANO: This was their only album that went to #1, so it obviously hit the core on something. I never blame a record for being too popular. Just like I do with David Bowie, I buy every compilation. I have all the songs ten times over, but I just love the fact that somebody put them in a new order. Richard has mixed and remixed these songs many times over the years. He's like a madman trying to polish up these songs to the point of their most definitive versions. I always thought that Karen was a singer like that, too. She had a sense of perfection about her. It's probably what killed her, but it really was part of their craft.

Performing "Sing" with a children's choir at the Hollywood Bowl.

7 HORIZON

Released June 6, 1975
Produced by Richard Carpenter
Associate Producer: Karen Carpenter
Recorded at A&M Studios, Hollywood, CA

Top Billboard Position: #13

RIAA Certification: Platinum

Singles:
"Please Mr. Postman" / "This Masquerade"
"Only Yesterday" / "Happy"
"Solitaire" / "Love Me for What I Am"

with Jeffrey de Hart, Quentin Harrison, Jan McDaniel, and Chris Tassin

Fans had gone two years without a new studio album when *Horizon* was released in June 1975. Less than thirty-five minutes long, the advances in sound quality more than made up for its brevity. The new and improved recording technology at A&M Studios (what was then state-of-the-art twenty-four-track recording) did not go unnoticed. Certified gold within two weeks of its release, *Horizon* went to #1 in Japan and the United Kingdom. In the United States, it peaked at a respectable #13.

By the summer of 1975 Karen's body had withered to just eighty-five pounds. She was proud of her svelte figure at first and purchased a new wardrobe to show it off. But when she walked out onstage in these low-cut silky gowns, some of which were strapless or even backless, there were gasps from the audience. Following a concert in New Haven, Harold Carpenter told a group of concerned friends, "She has anorexia nervosa," a little-known eating disorder he learned about in *Reader's Digest.*

At A&M Studios during the
Horizon sessions.

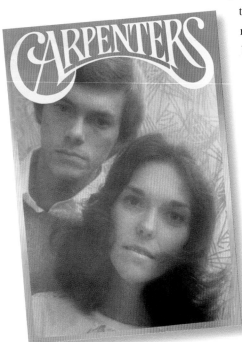

The quest to be thin began innocently after high school when Karen lost twenty-five pounds on the Stillman water diet. She maintained a healthy weight of 120 pounds until 1973 when she noticed a significant weight gain and vowed to "do something about it." Karen lost twenty pounds or so and by 1974 looked positively marvelous. But the dieting continued, and family and friends were alarmed by her unusual eating habits and emaciated appearance.

The firing of opening act Neil Sedaka that summer caused Karen's health to deteriorate rapidly. After several weeks at the Riviera in Las Vegas, she collapsed upon returning to Los Angeles. Karen's doctors said there was no way she could withstand the tours they had scheduled for Europe and Japan, so Richard and interim manager Terry Ellis flew to London and Tokyo to explain the cancellations. Under Agnes Carpenter's close watch, Karen slept fourteen to sixteen hours a day. Her weight eventually climbed to 104 pounds.

SCHMIDT: *Horizon* **was the most wanted album for this project. What made you want to discuss it?**

MCDANIEL: This album was a pivotal album for me, released just after I graduated from high school, and it's the last album by the Carpenters where I adored every note. It's significant in the sense that it was a coming-of-age album for them, and me as well.

DE HART: *Horizon* was a musical eureka moment for me. It had everything I could have ever dreamed of and hoped for in a Carpenters album. It was the pinnacle of their success in terms of songs, production, and even their image. For the first time they seemed like normal people, not just a contrived image that the record label was trying to manufacture.

TASSIN: *Horizon* is Richard and Karen at the top of their craft. It was one of the first Carpenters records I ever bought, and it remains my favorite to this day. Everything from the music to the design.

HARRISON: Out of all of their recordings, up to that point anyway, this one plays not only as the most cohesive but also as the most ambitious for the pair. If they're lucky, most artists have at least three to five albums where they get their creative chemistry right. *Horizon* came on the heels of several accomplished LPs, so it expressed an even smoother blend of lyric, vocal, and arrangement.

SCHMIDT: The album is bookended with "Aurora" and "Eventide," two brief music thoughts by John Bettis and Richard. Do you feel that those set the tone for or somehow framed the rest of the album?

DE HART: Those songs were most certainly the tone setters for the album. And they were sheer perfection. I honestly think they might be the best constructed of all the Carpenter-Bettis songs. John's lyrics were the most insightful and engaging of any he's written for them, including all the singles. It faded in, faded out, and was filled with all this amazing sound in between.

Adding strings to the new album.

MCDANIEL: Each song represented a horizon, one in the east as the sun was rising and the other in the west as the sun was setting. It created the perfect picture for what this album was going to be.

HARRISON: Karen is what makes these song pieces work. There's an underlying current of real-life experience and emotion driving the stirring melancholy in her vocal performance here. When she sings "weary to be home again," you just feel Karen's restlessness. It makes for some of the most gripping listening in the Carpenters canon.

TASSIN: Aurora means "the dawn," which went nicely with "You were the dawn breaking the night," the lyrics in "Only Yesterday." There's a recurring theme and it even ties into the beautiful and pensive cover photo of Karen and Richard standing out among the green foliage. That soft focus gives the look of early morning light.

SCHMIDT: "Only Yesterday" is a Carpenter-Bettis tune and one that really showcases Karen's range. It's been said that Richard and John thought of this as a 1960s-flavored song with the "wall of sound" in mind. Do you hear that?

HARRISON: I do. They created a lush retro-modern homage to the rock and roll/pop music of the Carpenters' youth. Erecting a

REVIEWS

"The grand, eloquent sound of their superb backup arrangements gives this act a special launching pad with which to catapult its vocal sound. . . . Karen's soft qualities plus her blending with brother Richard into an omni-directional attack provide easy to listen to material."
—*Billboard*

"It's certainly less than revolutionary to admit you like the Carpenters these days (in rock circles, if you recall, it formerly bordered on heresy). Everybody must be won over by now. . . . If all MOR were this good, one might not resent its all-out appropriation of the airwaves. . . . As for the Carpenters, they've transcended the genre and stand in a class by themselves."
—**Ken Barnes,** *Phonograph Record*

"*Horizon*, the Carpenters' most musically sophisticated album to date, smoothly adapts the spirit of mainstream Fifties pop to contemporary taste. . . . Against the carefully structured sound of the Carpenter formula, wherein Karen's solos burst in and out of diaphanous multi harmonies, Richard has imposed more elaborately orchestrated textures than before and wisely mixed them at a level that doesn't distract attention from Karen's intimately mixed singing."
—**Stephen Holden,** *Rolling Stone*

REFLECTIONS

"Postman" was #1 in three trades at the same time. The ideal thing would have been to put out the Horizon *album the week that "Postman" went to #1.*
—**Richard (1975)**

Please be assured that we did not fire Neil Sedaka for doing too well. In fact, we were delighted that he was receiving a nice response from the audience. It was a result of other circumstances of which he is totally aware that made it necessary for us to terminate his engagement. . . . It is a disappointment to us that he found it necessary to make statements concerning same to the press. Personally, the Las Vegas/Sedaka issue is an old matter, and right now I am much more concerned with Karen's health and writing new songs.
—**Richard (1975)**

Richard made Horizon *in the worst state I've ever seen him in. I mean we had got to a point where we didn't want to go to a studio. It was work, because we were so exhausted, and we've never had that. We've always been, "Hey, I can't wait to get into the studio," but that last album just drained everything, every drop of blood out of us. When it was done, we weren't glad it was done, we were upset with the way it turned out. Richard can work unbelievable hours, but this last time it was getting to us. But now it's gotta change. The two of us can't go on like that.*
—**Karen (1975)**

This business, as you know, brings a lot of pressures that artists never think about when they're trying to make it. There's a lot more to it than just walking on stage and singing. I wish it was just that because we really enjoy performing. . . . It really started catching up with Karen during the summer. She was starting to really get exhausted, losing her appetite, wanting to just turn in as soon as the concert was over, and started dropping a hell of a lot of weight. So by the time the first week of Vegas had passed, she was down to 86 pounds, which has to be between 40 or 45 pounds that she lost. It's way below what she should weigh.
Richard (1975)

Karen and I liked oldies. I like oldies and always thought that was a strong song. The Marvelettes did it originally in '61 and it was a #1 record. The Beatles covered it and did an excellent job with it. It's just a magical song. All it is is four chord changes. Karen just loved the idea of "Please Mr. Postman." For what it is, it's very very good. But I hate to say that the biggest selling Carpenters single worldwide to this day remains "Please Mr. Postman." I have to tell you that it's not one of my favorite Carpenters recordings.
—**Richard (1994)**

So you did certain things that you think will be a hit, but wished you'd never done, like "Please Mr. Postman." It's really an extremely well-performed and produced pop record. But we shouldn't have been doing any of those things (oldies) by that time. With side two of Now & Then, *that should have been it. And beyond that, the very few times that I chose to use a synthesizer, I have regretted it. Every last time.*
—**Richard (2009)**

new composition around Karen in this mold, they not only showcase their understanding of this bygone epoch, they do it justice by putting Karen's voice in this setup.

MCDANIEL: I've not heard that comment before, but I can see why one might say that. There was a layering or stacking of sounds. There's more than one electric piano, more than one guitar, and it's all layered together with the strings and the woodwinds.

TASSIN: There are so many layers in that song. There's the oboe echoing Karen with a yearning and bittersweet quality. That feels like what she's singing about.

DE HART: They really took advantage of all the new technology and upgrades at A&M Studios. They were exploring what they could do with twenty-four-track recording and really got into the technical end of things. This allowed them to spread their wings and fly.

SCHMIDT: Let's discuss "Desperado," which was a cover of the 1973 song by the Eagles.

DE HART: The Eagles, Linda Ronstadt, and Bonnie Raitt all performed their own versions, but the Carpenters recording would have been a hit if released as single. It's so easy to say that every song on this album could have been a single, but "Desperado" is one of Karen's most heart wrenching, emotive vocals. It's so well suited to her range and tailored to her voice.

On a smoke break with lyricist John Bettis.

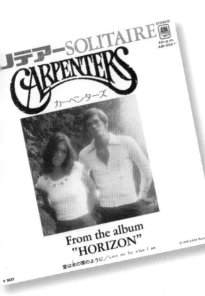

From the album
"HORIZON"

HARRISON: It's a respectful cover with an excellent vocal delivery from Karen. She takes this track right to the heart of its sadness and it's something to experience as a listener.

MCDANIEL: This was a new and more committed singing style from Karen. These were some of the higher notes that she'd ever sung and in what might be described as a full belt. She sang some notes on the chorus that we'd never heard from her this way before.

SCHMIDT: "Please Mr. Postman" had been released a year earlier, in 1974. It certainly wasn't their first venture into the oldies, but it was one of their first stand-alones, apart from a medley. And it gave them their third and final #1 on the Hot 100.

HARRISON: This is where the Carpenters tend to stumble and date themselves. Karen is competent here, but she doesn't sound particularly invigorating or invested. "Postman" is the only miss here on the album, but due to its solid production, it doesn't fragment the record overall.

MCDANIEL: This is one that I enjoyed, but it seemed like it was an intended hit. You could sense that the production decisions were made to appeal to a particular market. I saw it as a fine production, but not quite as high in artistic value as the other tracks on the album.

DE HART: I beg to differ. It was artistically immaculate. And as a high schooler who'd suffered years of abuse for being a Carpenters fan, this one brought it home for me. *Everybody* loved it. It was all over the radio and being played at all the school dances.

TASSIN: It's an impressive production and was so perfectly suited for radio. We hear the term "ear candy" applied to certain songs or recordings and this one deserves that term in the best way possible.

SCHMIDT: "I Can Dream Can't I" was their first attempt at a big standard from the Great American Songbook. Billy May was brought in to arrange the piece and to capture that 1940s big band sound. Chris, I remember that this is one of your all-time favorites.

TASSIN: This song took my love for Karen and the Carpenters to a new level. I first heard it when I was in grade school, going to sleep listening to my transistor radio, and this came on. I knew immediately who it was, but I had never heard anything quite so gorgeous in all my life. It's some of the most beautiful work she's ever done. The piece has a luxurious quality, and the nice thematic touch of having the album's title within its opening lyrics.

HARRISON: Karen is in such fine form here, and Richard's adaption of this classic is so gorgeous. This is a moment of brilliance for the Carpenters, no question.

DE HART: I *hated* it at first, but over time came to appreciate it. Now it's one of the best tracks on the album. It shows their versatility in musical styles. It also bucked a lot of trends and the expectations people had for them.

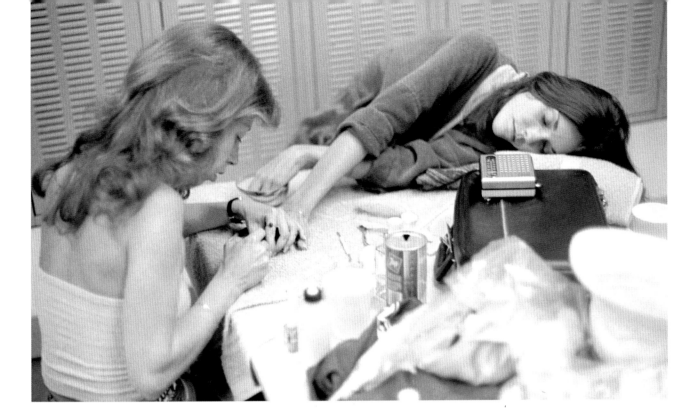

With stylist Sandy Holland for a manicure and nap between shows, 1975.

MCDANIEL: This song was a great touch and a perfect diversion, right smack in the middle of this album.

SCHMIDT: And they would work with Billy May again during the *Christmas Portrait* sessions. Let's talk about Neil Sedaka's "Solitaire." Richard always maintained it was one of Karen's finest performances, if not *the* finest. But Karen never particularly cared for it.

MCDANIEL: I agree with Richard. This is her finest performance on an album full of fine performances. It was probably due to the new and improved studio technology that they were able to capture the glorious colors of her voice and enhance them in a way they'd never done before. Richard's arrangement stays out of the way and we hear her exposed on the verses of this song. He switched from the Wurlitzer electric piano to a Fender Rhodes for this album. That gave it a different and fatter sound.

DE HART: One of their all-time best recordings, for sure. Every note is perfect. It's a tearjerker.

TASSIN: I agree. It's perfection from beginning to end. Richard's exquisite arrangement showcases her so well. And you can hear that they made great use of the new technology, particularly when it came to recording the drums in stereo.

MCDANIEL: One phrase that I played over and over again was in the second verse when she sang "goes up in smoke." The sound of her voice echoing with the steel guitar hovering in the background depicts a musical onomatopoeia of something going up in smoke.

HARRISON: "Solitaire" feels like the classic or seminal number on the LP. The arrangement is seamless, tailored for '70s AM pop radio, which was Richard's specialty. Karen is technically brilliant here, but I get the feeling this was more about singing the song

Soundcheck at the drums and
microphone, late 1975.

versus her actually feeling it. She comes across more engaged in
other spots on *Horizon*, notably "Happy."

**SCHMIDT: Speaking of "Happy," John Bettis collaborated with
guitarist Tony Peluso on that song. There's an interesting gambling
theme on this album, beginning with "Desperado" and the Queen
of Diamonds, then on "Solitaire," and now here on "Happy." And
there's an appearance on this song by the ARP Odyssey synthesizer.**

MCDANIEL: I didn't know this was an ARP, but this was their
first use of synthesizer. When I saw them on tour, Richard had a second keyboard above his grand piano, which he mostly used for the
string parts. It was probably an ARP Odyssey.

DE HART: Richard was so anti anything electronic, so it was a bit
of a surprise that the synth made its way onto this album. It's one of
my favorite songs, though. There's a reason *Billboard* and *Record Mirror*
said it was one of the best cuts on the album. Out of all the downbeat tearjerkers comes this upbeat, poppy song. I was ecstatic when
I flipped over the "Only Yesterday" single and heard this, but I wondered why it was a B-side when it should have been a single on its own.

HARRISON: I want to give "Happy" its due. It was the wild card
of the batch, that flash of subversive, creative brilliance suggesting
they could play outside of their own sound box and do something
really fresh. I wouldn't call this R&B, but it is certainly groovy. You
can tell Richard enjoyed setting up its to-and-fro vibe, and it's definitely a track about aural movement. You can hear that Karen is
enjoying herself here. Her smile, so to speak, comes through in her
performance.

**SCHMIDT: "(I'm Caught Between) Goodbye and I Love You" is
a Carpenter-Bettis tune that has a bit of a country feel to it with the
inclusion of the steel guitar.**

HARRISON: I really like this one. It has an affable or sympa-
thetic posture to its sound that as a listener you can't help but tune
in further as it spins.

DE HART: Classic. Another classic. They're *all* classics! This was
one of the songs I appreciated the most when it came out. I was
partial to the songs that Richard wrote for Karen. He selected all of
their songs with her voice in mind, of course, but it was obvious that
this one was written for it.

MCDANIEL: I'll be the devil's advocate here. I was always puzzled
by the end rhyme of the chorus: "This double life you've handed me

is like the devil and the deep blue sea." That was not an expression I was familiar with. Perhaps it was a cultural literacy issue.

DE HART: I never thought about that before. But Ella Fitzgerald recorded a song called "Between the Devil and the Deep Blue Sea" in 1947. And Frank Sinatra recorded it in 1987.

MCDANIEL: Oh, OK. That's probably an example of John Bettis's rich song heritage coming out.

SCHMIDT: "Love Me for What I Am" seems like it could be a companion piece to the previous song. It's a Bettis lyric with music by Palma Pascale.

DE HART: *Billboard* got this one right, too. It's one of the best songs on the album. It's also Tony Peluso's best solo, even better than "Goodbye to Love," in my opinion.

HARRISON: I like the power ballad guitar center as well, which the Carpenters were responsible for coining in many respects.

MCDANIEL: It's a really terrific pop song and one I'm surprised hasn't had more legs. This is one of those arrangements in which Richard devoted the entire first verse to just piano and voice, allowing Karen to really be heard.

HARRISON: My feeling about this song is that Richard selected it specifically for Karen. Growing up in such a emotionally stifled home, the Carpenters didn't really discuss their personal affairs among themselves like they should have. I interpret this song as Richard trying to reach out and empower his sister to stand tall as a young woman, despite her innate struggles. In turn, Karen picks up that emotional frequency and turns in a powerful performance.

TASSIN: The lyric has her speaking to someone, but it has an introspective quality as well. She was such a great interpreter. Karen's voice on *Horizon* has the usual beauty and richness, but there's also an authoritative and majestic quality to it on this album. It's almost as if she is a celestial being with all the answers and the ability to be the balm for our hearts.

MCDANIEL: As far as an exhibition of Karen's skills, the *Horizon* album is the best. It's not the best Carpenters album, in my opinion, but as far as a showcase of what made her special, this one is it. I understand that Richard and Karen were absolutely exhausted throughout the entire process of making this album, but I don't hear that at all. I hear nothing but superb artistry and honesty shining through. It had never happened quite like this before, and it never happened again in the same way. This is as close to perfect as a recorded voice can be.

TASSIN: It's a masterwork. I agree that never before and never again did it all come together for their talents like it did on *Horizon*.

(opposite)
An outtake from the *Horizon* photo sessions.

8 A KIND OF HUSH

Released June 11, 1976
Produced by Richard Carpenter
Associate Producer: Karen Carpenter
Recorded at A&M Studios, Hollywood, CA

Top Billboard Position: #33

RIAA Certification: Gold

Singles:
"There's a Kind of Hush" / "(I'm Caught
Between) Goodbye and I Love You"
"I Need to Be in Love" / "Sandy"
"Goofus" / "Boat to Sail"

with Michael Lansing, Patrick Summers, and Mark Taft

January 1, 1976, brought a new year, a new recording contract with A&M Records, and a new manager, entertainment mogul Jerry Weintraub. Attempting to prioritize the activities of their professional lives, Weintraub decided to limit the number of concerts the Carpenters would perform each year. It was his feeling that they were primarily a recording act and should have ample time to work in the studio.

Fatigue and health issues plagued their next album release, *A Kind of Hush,* which failed to reach the Top 30 and marked the beginning of their descent in popularity. Even Karen's favorite song, "I Need to Be in Love," fell short of the Top 20, and the oddball "Goofus" peaked at #56, their lowest-charting single to that point. *A Kind of Hush* eventually went gold, but it was not the commercial success of previous Carpenters albums.

Building on changes established by Terry Ellis during his brief stint as interim manager, Jerry Weintraub revamped the Carpenters'

tired stage show format from the ground up. He called on the expertise of the writing/directing team of Ken and Mitzi Welch as well as famed Broadway choreographer Joe Layton to give the show some pizazz.

Karen's role as a drummer became more of a novelty and was relegated to play only on a Gerwshin medley drum feature. Wearing blue jeans and her iconic "Lead Sister" T-shirt, she ran around the stage showing off on a battery of percussion instruments. To highlight Richard's importance, he entered to "Ladies and gentlemen, Mr. Richard Carpenter" and briefly conducted the orchestra. A large mirror was hung above his grand piano to spotlight his playing.

SCHMIDT: I have heard *A Kind of Hush* called melancholy, sleepy, and soft. *Horizon* was soft but still had some edge to it. This album was the first that seemed to cross over into "easy listening" territory. Do you think the album title is fitting?

TAFT: It's very fitting. I love this album. It was released in June but doesn't feel like a summer disc in either look or sound. It feels like fall to me. I just love the entire packaging of it, from top to bottom. Overall, it's a very traditional feminine album. Compared to their prior records, this doesn't seem as much like a duo. Richard seems to be way in the background. The title is fitting, but I don't think it's an insult. When I've heard it called "A Kind of Mush," now *that's* an insult.

At the American Music Awards, where they presented the award for *Favorite Pop Single* to Glen Campbell for "Rhinestone Cowboy," January 31, 1976.

SUMMERS: I tend to think of the Carpenters albums, at least those after *Now & Then*, to not be so thematically linked. They seemed to be wanting to do a variety and cover a lot of bases. For me, *Horizon* is *the* great Carpenters album, but I love *A Kind of Hush*. I don't think of it as one thing. I really think of it as a full meal. There's meat and potatoes and desert and everything, but not so much one idea.

LANSING: It's a sad album for me to listen to now. The songs had tender moments. "You," "Can't Smile Without You," and "I Need to Be in Love" all had that flavor of writing your emotions on the cuff of your sleeve. For me, this album stood out as something that really struck right into your heart when you listened to it. And we hear much less of Richard's vocal on this album, except for the last cut, "Breaking Up Is Hard to Do." You can tell he had fun with that.

SUMMERS: There's a lot of '60s retro stuff on the *A Kind of Hush* album. And it always struck me that, in the mid-'70s, there was already nostalgia for the '60s. It felt like they were going back to their roots on *A Kind of Hush* with

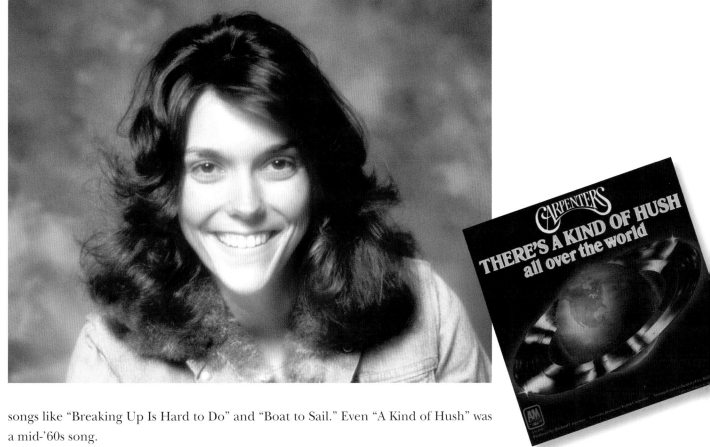

songs like "Breaking Up Is Hard to Do" and "Boat to Sail." Even "A Kind of Hush" was a mid-'60s song.

LANSING: It was retro. Richard was all about muscle cars from the '50s and '60s, so a lot of his love of that whole genre spilled over into their music, especially on this album.

SCHMIDT: The title song was also the album's first single. "There's a Kind of Hush (All Over the World)" was the last in the duo's string of sixteen-consecutive Top 20 hits, a run started with "Close to You" in 1970. They'd had success with oldies on side two of their *Now & Then* album, then "Postman" had given them a #1 on the *Billboard* Top 100. What was it about the Carpenters and oldies?

SUMMERS: There was such a reaction against hard rock and to groups like the Rolling Stones. That was a pretty new phenomenon. The Carpenters were already

In the courtyard at the historic Grauman's Chinese Theatre in Hollywood, July 19, 1976.

retro in sound when they appeared, but so many people were longing for that, especially the postwar people who were aging at that time. They were in their thirties and forties and the Carpenters allowed them to still feel a part of popular music in a way that the Rolling Stones and other groups like that did not. They were very alienating for middle America. The Carpenters weren't. That was certainly the case with my family. I was thirteen years old and a budding musician when *A Kind of Hush* came out. My parents were worried about the effect of rock music, but they weren't worried about me buying Carpenters records.

SCHMIDT: It was around this time that the Carpenters changed management. Jerry Weintraub brought in the directing and writing team of Ken and Mitzi Welch, as well as Broadway director and choreographer Joe Layton to revamp their image and stage show.

LANSING: I had the luxury of seeing the show and being a part of their stage show, before and after the revamp. Joe Layton walked into the room on the first day of rehearsal and asked if everyone had their pencils. We all scrambled to find one. He said, "Hold them out in front of you." Everyone had a pencil, including Karen and Richard, so we were all students of Joe Layton. "The pencil is your ego," he said. "OK, time to drop the pencil. *That* was your ego. I am going to ask you to do things that will make you uncomfortable. This is not about being comfortable. This is about creating a cohesive new show for Richard and Karen and we are *all* going to do our best."

TAFT: The first time I ever saw them was 1976 at the Riviera with David Brenner as the opening act. I remember, musically, the anticipation after Richard came out and before Karen appeared. You could feel it in the crowd. It was electrifying!

SCHMIDT: Karen's voice changed with this album. How would you describe her new sound?

TAFT: It grabbed me in a different way. It was less power, less push, less dark and husky. It was gentle and tender. Introspective and sensual. I heard "Boat to Sail" and realized the girl next door is growing up. But there were also times I thought it sounded as if her spirit had been broken. Like she had been through it. I didn't really follow her

personal life much during those years. I was a teenager. But I sensed something was missing.

SUMMERS: There was more depth to the singing and more connection to the words and music in *A Kind of Hush*. It was deeper in every way. With this album Karen became more of an actress-singer, than just a singer. There was more of a narrative quality to the singing. And she had such a distinctive voice. Working in opera, as I do, the thing one looks for in a singer is a sonic imprint. You can tell who it is in just one note. All of the great popular singers had that as well, but no one ever had a more distinct sonic imprint than Karen Carpenter. You knew who it was immediately.

LANSING: One day I was driving Karen to A&M and she started singing. I told her that she didn't need to sing quietly because of me. "Just sing how you normally do," I said. "This is how I sing," she told me. I couldn't believe it. "You're kidding me!" I said. "I've been running your monitors on stage and I had no idea!" She sang so beautifully, so breathy, never pushing it. She knew her instrument well and knew how to get the most from it. Whether it was tone quality or emotion, Karen had it down.

Backstage at the Sahara, Lake Tahoe, California, 1976.

SCHMIDT: "You" was a Randy Edelman tune. The Carpenters seemed to do well with his songs, having recorded "I Can't Make Music" and "Piano Picker" on previous albums.

TAFT: This should have been the third single off the album. It was much stronger than "Goofus," as far as radio friendliness goes.

SUMMERS: The arching sort of lyricism and yearning in that song makes it one of my favorite Carpenters performances. It's my favorite track on the album. It's so simple, musically, but so sophisticatedly performed. The text of the song is joyous, but she illuminates it with such underlying yearning and longing that it's a very ambiguous song. She went so deeply into the material. It's the performance of a great actress, even though you can't see her.

SCHMIDT: The song "Sandy" was apparently an ode from John Bettis to the Carpenters' hairdresser Sandy Holland. It features some beautiful harmonies and has always been one of Richard's favorites. Thoughts on this one?

TAFT: Some guys will do anything to get the girl! Nice flute work by Bob Messenger and Tom Scott on this one. Karen sounds great as always, but this song only reinforces the album's lightweight reputation. This is the kind of music their critics always accused them of making.

SUMMERS: A simplistic strophic song that has a saccharine and unmemorable arrangement a lá "Mister Rogers' Neighborhood." It feels very hastily done. I've always been confused by the lyric: "though I've been in love before, it wasn't with you." Who is the voice of the song? Sandy seems to be the answer to all problems, but is Sandy really the object of the song, or is the "you" sung about somebody else? It's probably the weakest track on an otherwise enjoyable album.

SCHMIDT: Let's discuss "Goofus" now. Talk about an oldie! I am one of only a few fans I know that loves it. It shouldn't have been a single, but let's just talk about it as a recording on an album. To me, it's almost a nod to the zany novelty songs they grew up listening to in their father's collection of 78s.

SUMMERS: It's one of those songs that made our parents' generation, the World War II generation, feel OK about liking a "rock" band. It's the music of their youth, a 1930s song. It was comfort food.

TAFT: It was probably more fitting for an album release than if they'd recorded a Spike Jones type of song. There's more melody and it's not as frantic. It's playful and I can hear the self-parody in it, but it sort of cemented that they were out of step with what was going on around them.

SUMMERS: Well, they *were* out of step with what was going on around them. Richard Carpenter was a more serious musician than most people who were out in front of the public in popular music at the time.

With their entourage, 1976.

REVIEWS

"Exceptionally pretty album, with even more emphasis on Karen Carpenter's versatile, excellent vocals than in past efforts. Soft, easy ballads filled with the lush production of Richard Carpenter dominate the set, though the material alternates from the straight ballad form to easy rock to almost vaudevillian material to supper club, piano bar styled music. Keyboards handled well by Richard, who has always taken somewhat of a backseat when it comes to performing but does as good a job of production as anyone in the business. . . . One of the true legitimate super acts."
—*Billboard*

"The dynamic duo of the MOR/easy listening idiom have come up with another winner. *A Kind of Hush* is a clean collection of tunes that is truly representative of the kind of music that the Carpenters are famous for—smooth, ingratiating melodies that bear their contemporary trademark."
—*Cashbox*

"The Carpenters have always displayed good taste, and musicians of such caliber don't suddenly lose that quality. This is in no sense a bad album. But the Carpenters are victims, in a sense, of establishing their own enormously high standards—perhaps we now expect every new release to eclipse, or even match, the astonishingly high standards of their past. . . . The Carpenters are enduring artists whose talent will span generations. Let's assume this uneventful album doesn't amount to anything beyond a temporary loss of energy."
—Ray Coleman, *Melody Maker*

"You may have noticed that a kind of hush fell over the world recently. It was a wonderful sight to see. Everyone laid down their arms and joined hands as brothers and sisters. The reason for this somewhat monumental world event was the release of the new album by the Carpenters, the ultimate brother and sister. The album is appropriately titled *A Kind of Hush* (A&M), and at this point it is the odds-on favorite to win the Grammy, the Nobel Peace Prize and the Reader's Digest Sweepstakes."
—Joel McNally, *Milwaukee Journal*

"As usual, the production, the charts, and the engineering are all absolutely superb and sound like a cool million—a figure that the Carpenters probably have an easy familiarity with by now. Their fans—and oh man, are they legion—will eat it up, of course. But, even served in the finest bone china, it's still m-u-s-h."
—*Stereo Review*

REFLECTIONS

We have a new outlook; there's a new feeling of happiness and enjoyment. We've begun a new Carpenters era.
—Richard (1976)

This is a keyboard band, basically. I figure I'm there to complement the keyboards behind Karen's vocal. I guess that would not suit most guitarists who seem to figure the guitar is the lead instrument, but when you are working in the studios with Richard, it's like an apprenticeship. He and Karen are very energetic and determined people to work for, and I love it. They'll work hard and long for hours to get the slightest thing right, and it's exhausting, but it's tremendous discipline. Some people criticize the Carpenters' sound as cold and lacking something, but that's probably because it's so precise.
—Tony Peluso, guitarist (1976)

I think my favorite today is "I Need to Be in Love." That really upsets me when I hear it. I've had so many ladies call me on the phone and say, "That is my song." So many have the empathy. It really hits me right at home. Certain nights on the stage, it really upsets me. I sing it and I'm almost putting myself into tears. It's so personal because John Bettis, our lyricist, wrote that. . . . The first verse of that says, "The hardest thing I've ever done is keep believing there's someone in this crazy world for me / The way that people come and go through temporary lives / My chance could come and I might never know." And I said, "Oh, my God, it's so true!"
—Karen (1976)

Our music shouldn't be compared to rock. It's pop, and it's progressive in its own pop way. We're not your average "easy-listening" act by any means. Easy-listening artists will only record what has already been done.
—Richard (1976)

We expected it. It can't stay at that level. It just can't. Karen and I knew that sooner or later things were going to be settling down a bit. And that's exactly what they did. . . . We were still well-known, we could do good concert business, we had our recording contract, our albums still did well, they just didn't do millions of units the way they had done. So it wasn't the end of the world.
—Richard (1986)

"Lead Sister" at the Hippodrome in Birmingham, England, November 20, 1976.

SCHMIDT: "Can't Smile Without You" was a huge hit for Barry Manilow in 1978. Could it have been a hit for Carpenters in 1976 if they'd released it as a single?

LANSING: Barry found the magic in that song. Maybe it was just the largeness of Barry that could pull it off a little bit differently than the Carpenters. Everything was big with Barry.

SCHMIDT: "I Need to Be in Love" was the album's second single and one that surprised a lot of listeners. Was it the addition of the OK Chorale studio singers? Commercially, it seemed to mark the beginning of the end for them.

TAFT: It's kind of mixed for me. I wish they would have dropped the OK Chorale and just used them for Christmas recordings. Someone once said that "I Need to Be in Love" had an almost spiritual quality to it. I wonder if the OK Chorale was responsible for that. This should have been the "Rainy Days and Mondays" of the album. It feels like it should have had some bite and maybe a melancholy harmonica or something else. Still, I don't think John Bettis ever crafted more compelling lyrics for her to sing. It's powerful.

SUMMERS: It always struck me as a Broadway eleven o'clock number. That's the song ten minutes from the end of the show where the character changes everything about themselves. It always struck me as that. If it didn't do so well, it may be because it made people emotionally uncomfortable because it was too intimate. Suddenly we had to think about Karen Carpenter as a human—a woman—instead of Karen Carpenter, the artist.

LANSING: To me it's the song that Karen wrote. She didn't write it, but she sings it like it's her own. Obviously, John was close enough to both to know exactly what to write.

SCHMIDT: "One More Time" is a standout on this album, almost in a different league. It makes such a beautiful statement in its simplicity.

TAFT: Richard's restraint in the orchestration was the absolute right thing to do with this song. I always heard it as a companion piece to Ray Price's "For the Good Times." It had that same sort of feel.

SCHMIDT: Karen and Richard heard "Boat to Sail" on Jackie DeShannon's *New Arrangement* album.

TAFT: This is my favorite song on the album. Karen's vocal is stellar. Richard's piano playing reminds me of "This Masquerade." I was learning to sail with some neighbors around the time the album came out, so my worlds converged. This was one of those driving down Pacific Coast Highway in a convertible kind of songs.

SCHMIDT: "I Have You" always stood out to me because of Karen's double-tracking on the chorus. Although they were masters at multilayered recordings and the overdubbing process, this is one of the few instances where she really just duets with herself.

SUMMERS: At heart, Richard's brilliance as an arranger is because he has such a choral mind. Richard's arrangements, including this one, have affected an entire generation of classical musicians, like me. That's the kind of music we deal with all the time. There are duets and people singing together. That they perfected Karen singing with herself, especially in such a gorgeous, simple, and to-the-point arrangement, is just genius.

SCHMIDT: What are your thoughts on the Carpenters closing *A Kind of Hush* with one of Neil Sedaka's signature tunes, "Breaking Up Is Hard to Do," just a year after he was fired as their opening act? Was this a statement of further resentment or were they trying to make nice?

On stage in New York, 1976.

SUMMERS: They *must* have been trying to make nice. They had endless possibilities as far as what they could have recorded. Why put a famous Neil Sedaka song on there if they weren't trying to make amends?

LANSING: I thought it was kind of odd that they recorded the song. That Sedaka-Vegas fiasco was an uncomfortable situation. And it was caused by Neil, not the Carpenters. The balance had flip-flopped. Neil wouldn't get off the stage. He was eating it up because he hadn't seen this kind of crowd in a long time. It was because of this unfortunate incident, along with his good fortune and great songs, that Neil's career skyrocketed. But Richard did what he needed to do to make things right. When you're the headliner and something is not right in a show, you must *make* it right.

UK-released *Live at the Palladium*, recorded in London, November 1976.

9 PASSAGE

Released September 23, 1977
Produced by Richard Carpenter
Associate Producer: Karen Carpenter
Recorded at A&M Studios, Hollywood, CA

Top Billboard Position: #49

Singles:
"All You Get from Love Is a Love Song" / "I
Have You"
"Calling Occupants of Interplanetary Craft" /
"Can't Smile Without You"
"Sweet, Sweet Smile" / "I Have You"

with David Konjoyan, Tom Nolan, and Matt Wallace

On *A Kind of Hush*, Karen and Richard lacked much of the determination and energy present in their earlier efforts. They also found it more difficult to write and select material that listeners would buy and radio programmers would play. It stands to reason that it was through experimentation, exploration, and even a little desperation that the Carpenters' next studio album, *Passage*, was born.

The recording of two songs on *Passage* turned into media events. For "Calling Occupants of Interplanetary Craft," a cover of the spacey song by the Canadian group Klaatu, Karen and Richard brought in arranger and orchestrator Peter Knight, an Englishman known for his work on the Moody Blues' *Days of Future Passed* album.

Knight also arranged and conducted "Don't Cry for Me, Argentina," the sweeping ballad from Andrew Lloyd Webber's *Evita*. Los Angeles–area news outlets were invited to witness the colossal recording session, which gathered more than one hundred instrumentalists and fifty

(previous page)
Posing for photographer Harry Langdon, November 4, 1977.

chorus members on A&M's Chaplin Stage. Due to contractual agreements, the Los Angeles Philharmonic was humorously credited as the "Overbudget Philharmonic" in the album's liner notes.

"Sweet, Sweet Smile," the final *Passage* single, took aim at the Country Music charts where it made the US Top 10. It was also issued with "Reason to Believe," "Jambalaya," and "Top of the World" as a four-song promo *Country Collection* EP, which was sent to radio stations and regional promoters. Karen and Richard contemplated an all-country album, but A&M's Jerry Moss was quick to remind them that another traditional pop album should be their priority.

While the Carpenters considered *Passage* a creative success, it was a commercial flop, becoming their first album to fall short of gold status. Fickle American audiences left them scratching their heads, but the duo's presence on the international music scene remained strong. "Calling Occupants of Interplanetary Craft" was a huge hit in Japan, while "Sweet, Sweet Smile" was a smash in Germany.

Arriving at the ABC-TV Affiliates Party, March 13, 1977 at the Century Plaza Hotel.

SCHMIDT: This was one of the least popular albums among the commentators. What made you want to discuss this album for this project?

WALLACE: I'd been a Carpenters fan for quite a while when I heard "Calling Occupants of Interplanetary Craft" on the radio. That really intrigued me, so I picked up the *Passage* album. It was one of the most eclectic things they'd ever done. They cut a wide swath of different types of music and tried to push a lot of boundaries. I thought this could be the chrysalis for them opening to new musical adventures.

KONJOYAN: At the time it came out, this album was a significant departure. I think the Carpenters really viewed this as a turning point in their careers and staked a claim that they could do some new and different things.

NOLAN: It *is* an eclectic album, undeniably, and it reminds me now of their first album, *Offering*, in that it goes in a lot of different directions and tries a lot of different

With parents Agnes and Harold during the Concours d'Elegance at the Long Beach Grand Prix, April 3, 1977.

approaches. It's reflective of different kinds of music that were popular and oncoming at that time in the late 1970s. I'm not sure that I'm as excited about the results, although it's certainly a worthwhile album. They were trying to do different things, but it was due in part to their frustrations as artists.

SCHMIDT: This was the first Carpenters album to not contain any original material. The lackluster chart performance of *A Kind of Hush* left them desperate for a hit. Does it seem with this album that they were trying to experiment with just about every possible genre in hopes that one would stick?

NOLAN: In a way yes, but I don't know if they were trying to find one specific direction. A lot of artists lost their way in trying to stay fresh and contemporary, and they weren't the only ones trying to make their way through this complicated decade. Some of the things worked, some didn't. One frustration for me is that Karen is buried under a lot of fussy sonics and the arrangements are not as interesting as they ought to be.

WALLACE: There is literally as much instrumental music as there is Karen singing. Some of the instrumentals just meander all over the place and it feels like a sailboat without a sail. But that said, I do like that they let go of the steering wheel to an extent and I'm drawn to this record because they pushed boundaries. This feels like a distant cousin to U2's approach to their *Achtung Baby* album, where they let go and basically said, "OK, we're not going to be U2 anymore. Let's try to be something else."

KONJOYAN: Listening to this album again in 2018 and reflecting, it struck me as them deliberately going off in a different direction. And it strikes me as a well-intentioned overreaction to *A Kind of Hush*, which was the Carpenters at their softest, most pristine sound. I think they were trying to find material that would strike a lot of people as unlikely, with "Calling Occupants" being the epitome of that.

May 24, 1977, with more than a hundred instrumentalists and the 50-voice Gregg Smith Singers on the A&M soundstage during the recording of "Don't Cry for Me, Argentina."

SCHMIDT: The album opens with the Michael Franks tune, "B'wana She No Home." This was one of several "live cuts" on the album and featured Pete Jolly on piano and Tom Scott on sax. What did the designation of being a "live cut" mean?

WALLACE: "Live" in the studio usually means the basic tracks are done live with everyone in the room and interacting with one another at once. The vocals are almost always done afterward because people tend to agonize over them. Anyhow, I went through and added up this stuff. There're forty-two bars of Karen singing and fifty-six bars of flute solo, two sax solos, and a piano solo. Big mistake. What Karen was doing was so beautiful, and all the other instrumental soloing just got in the way. A second sax solo, are you kidding? OK, I'll get off my soapbox.

KONJOYAN: I have to say, after that comment, I quit this conversation! Well, I didn't add up any bars, so Matt has that on me. But "B'wana" is one of the songs that really works on the album. It's not totally outside their wheelhouse, and she sounds good on the song. It feels like it meanders some. Or perhaps the whole album meanders, but I wonder if that's the point. This album feels like it had the sprawl of a double-album that was just a single album. It calls to mind albums like *Sandinista!* by the Clash and other epic albums that failed as much as they succeeded. *Passage* is probably the closest the Carpenters got to doing something like that.

NOLAN: This was an attempt to produce a more sophisticated album. As you note, perhaps opening the album with this long track with a jazz feel was an attempt to present themselves in a new context and present Karen in a more mature and polished manner. I don't welcome the results, particularly, but perhaps they wanted to showcase some other aspects of their talent.

WALLACE: I loved it. The moment I put on "B'wana" I was absolutely thrilled because I loved the vibe and everything about it. I felt that Karen's vocal approach was sexy and playful and groovy. They could have shortened this song and possibly put another song on the record, or even replaced one of the many instrumental solos with

Karen doing some vocal scatting. If you want to push boundaries and be jazzy, let her scat and see what happens. It's possible that she might have come up with something really inspired.

SCHMIDT: "All You Get from Love Is a Love Song" is one of the more traditional Carpenters songs on the album, but it sounded more ambitious and energetic than anything on their previous album.

KONJOYAN: I agree with that. It was certainly more upbeat than what they'd done in the recent past and I do think it's a very good song. In their prime, this would have been a Top 10 hit.

NOLAN: It's a polished cut and the vocal is good. It's lyrical and it is one of the more Karen-accessible tracks on the album.

WALLACE: This is a stunning vocal. It's immediate, very organic, and in your face.

SCHMIDT: Another traditional Carpenters song, "I Just Fall in Love Again," would have likely guaranteed them a hit, but they were really trying to push the envelope this

At the Long Beach Grand Prix.

REVIEWS

"From the opening cut to the final track, this album represents the Carpenters' most boldly innovative and sophisticated undertaking yet. The title is indicative of the album's journey into the musical spectrum, as the material constantly shifts gears from calypso, lustily orchestrated complex pop rhythms, jazz flavored ballads, reggae and melodic, upbeat numbers."
—*Billboard*

"After all these years of admiring their excellence, we have come to expect something special from Carpenters albums. This one just will not do. . . . They are still floundering amid gimmicks which do not suit them, and Karen's melting vocals—always their most powerful asset—are lost when they tackle 'Man Smart, Woman Smarter' and 'Don't Cry for Me, Argentina.' . . . It's a tragic comment on such talent, but Carpenters fans can safely ignore this release; let's wish them a speedy return to musical decisiveness."
—**Ray Coleman,** *Melody Maker*

"You get this image of Richard (who chooses and arranges this wide variety of material) searching frantically for the most unlikely stuff to do, and then, Karen singing it just like Karen Carpenter. . . . As bizarre as some of the material is, Carpenters fans will be pleased with the result. The cynical music critics still won't take them seriously."
—**Joel McNally,** *Milwaukee Journal*

"The Carpenters' latest album is nothing if not adventurous. . . . The program concludes rather remarkably with a science-fiction song, 'Calling Occupants of Interplanetary Craft,' which manages to avoid resorting to a single sound-effects cliché. There are, it's true, also a number of more characteristically mild Carpenters items, such as 'I Just Fall in Love Again' and 'Sweet, Sweet Smile,' but by and large *Passage* is an eventful recording."
—*Stereo Review*

REFLECTIONS

A lot of different types of material went around and round. And we just got a lot more involved, not only with product and material but with sound. And different ways to get different sounds. Just trying all these different things was really a challenge.
—**Karen (1977)**

When recording, we usually begin with bass, drums, piano, and build from there. But on several of these tracks, almost the whole thing was recorded live all at once. Certain pieces call for that. . . . When we brought in all these pieces [for "Don't Cry for Me Argentina"], we didn't know if it would work, but we wanted to do it in a big way. And we wanted an orchestra which plays all the time rather than studio musicians.
—**Richard (1977)**

I'm a Beatles fan, a Klaatu fan, and a science fiction fan. For "Occupants," Klaatu employed a lot of sound effects—tape delay, things like that—and did all their sweetening with synthesizer. I wanted to use the real thing.
—**Richard (1977)**

We always try to get one country song on our albums. Not for any specific purpose but because we like it. We don't go in and say we've got to record a song that will get on the country charts. We always just go in with what we like. . . . And it's not like we didn't do country before.
—**Karen (1978)**

For the last three years there has been a definite resistance to our product, and I don't know why. We've been doing our best to turn out the finest product we can. Richard keeps changing direction. We've covered practically every aspect that is capable of being put to disc with the exception of classical. We haven't done that yet.
—**Karen (1978)**

We just don't know what Top 40 radio is looking for. One minute they say they're looking for a traditional Carpenters record. We give them one of those and they don't want it. They say they want something different, so we give them "Occupants" and they don't want that either. We give them country and Top 40 again resists. If somebody would just let us know what the problem is, then we could take it from there. Everybody has a different answer.
—**Karen (1978)**

I don't see Passage *as all that different. We were comfortable doing every one of those songs. It's true, "Calling Occupants of Interplanetary Craft" had the spacey noises, but the core of the song is like one of our rhythm ballads. It wasn't like we were trying to find a new audience, because we love our audience. I still like that album a great deal.*
—**Richard (1981)**

time around. Anne Murray had a Top 20 Country hit with it in 1979. Do you think Karen and Richard missed the boat not releasing this as a single?

NOLAN: It's a shame that they didn't. Again, this is one of the strongest tracks. It's very likable and her voice is front and center. What grandiosity there is in the chart is in service to the vocal and doesn't get in the way.

KONJOYAN: I have a different take on this song. I do think she sounds great, as she always does on these kinds of songs, but releasing it as a single would've been exactly what they didn't want to do at that time. They were trying to break away from that with this album.

WALLACE: I agree. Releasing that as a single would have gone against the grain of what they were trying to accomplish. It's nice to have it as a touchstone in the middle this record, but to release it would've set them back. I'm glad they didn't release it as a single, but I'm also glad it's on the record because it's lovely.

Karen, age 27.

SCHMIDT: There are several "event" songs on this album. "Don't Cry for Me Argentina" from the rock opera *Evita* is one of them. They brought in Peter Knight from England to orchestrate and some 150 people assembled on A&M's soundstage for the recording. What do you think their goal was with an epic performance such as this?

KONJOYAN: The musical was happening at the time. This was a grandiose piece of music to tackle and it added another genre to this album, but I'm not a fan of it.

WALLACE: I'm with you. I'm not a huge fan of the song, but I like that Karen's voice is naked. There's nothing obscuring it and it's beautiful. As a technical production it's exciting, but as a listener it just left me flat.

NOLAN: I suspect it was the notion of presenting Karen in a different context. It's a sort of dramatic stunt and a way of saying, "Look what else she can do!" Like Aretha Franklin doing Puccini. It seemed like a good idea at the time, but nobody cares about this song. It doesn't have any meaning out of the context of the play. A big thing with Richard was to be taken seriously as a producer, a song chooser, a songwriter, and a record maker. And he certainly deserved to be. But some of these later decisions were problematic.

WALLACE: I'm not crazy about the album artwork, either. The person who did it was a fine artist, but it's not reflective of his normal style. Their picture isn't even on there. You pick it up and it doesn't say BUY ME, even to Carpenters fans.

KONJOYAN: It's interesting that you bring that up. I had the same thoughts. The album cover isn't very exciting. It was done by

Filming "Sweet, Sweet Smile" for the *Space Encounters* television special, early April 1978.

Lou Beach, who did a lot of interesting stuff for A&M, but this just left me a little flat. Also, the Carpenters logo is tiny and on the back of the cover, which struck me as very deliberate.

WALLACE: It's not my favorite album cover, but I understand why they did it. It reflects the musical direction that they were trying to capture on this record.

SCHMIDT: Let's flip to side two now. Karen wasn't usually a song chooser, but she did find Juice Newton's "Sweet, Sweet Smile," which gave them a Top 10 crossover hit on the Country charts.

KONJOYAN: "Sweet, Sweet Smile" is great. I didn't know that Karen had picked it, but it's a really great choice. It almost sounds like she picked it, though, because she's singing it with a joy that we don't hear on the rest of this album. Come to think of it, you don't hear that on a lot of the other albums. Singing with joy wasn't necessarily her calling card, but she could do it and did it well. It's one of the stronger on the album.

NOLAN: It's just about irresistible. It's a wonderful track and she's front and center and full of joy and bounce. The guitar solo is nice, too. It's just wonderful all the way around.

SCHMIDT: "Two Sides" is classic Carpenters. It sounds like it could have been on *Horizon* several years earlier.

KONJOYAN: It's one of the stronger songs on the album. It almost feels folkish or something in the singer-songwriter vein. Lee Ritenour is playing guitar on it. The song has a great sentiment and an interesting lyric. I was struck with the way she kind of sails out at the end of the song when she sings "goodbye." I really love listening to it.

NOLAN: A very nice track and one with single potential. It's a very compelling song and you want to hear it repeatedly.

SCHMIDT: "Man Smart, Woman Smarter" is one of the few Carpenters songs I skip. I appreciate most of their novelty songs, but this one's lost on me. An interesting side note, though, is that Leon Russell played piano on this one.

WALLACE: It's a terrific song, but it's a boilerplate, textbook example of how not to produce a song in that it completely obscures the vocalist. There were so many bird tweets and whistles and saws and bubble sounds, which took a song that could have had some backbone and some grit and made it really *cute* instead. This was a missed-opportunity track. It was just way too busy. And if you're going to have Leon Russell on your song, you'd better be sure you can hear him. Instead of all those chirps and bleeps and bloops, let Leon Russell play some riffs here and there.

KONJOYAN: Richard was a Spike Jones fan and this kind of feels like their Spike Jones take on the song. It was probably meant to convey a sense of humor. He wanted to be taken seriously but not *always* seriously. But just for the record, I skip over this song, too.

NOLAN: "Man Smart, Woman Smarter" is one of those where her vocals are buried. And it's not the greatest song. If they wanted to do a novelty song or something clever, why not do a Harry Nilsson song? I was at one of their recording sessions and Karen came in singing "Kojak Columbo." She said, "Doesn't Harry Nilsson write great songs?" Why wasn't *he* on this album?

SCHMIDT: The other epic/event song on *Passage* is "Calling Occupants of Interplanetary Craft," which Richard heard on an album by the Beatles-influenced group Klaatu. It was a timely release with all the *Close Encounters* and *Star Wars* mania of the late 1970s, Tom, I love that you called this "Charles Ives goes to Mars" back then.

NOLAN: Did I now? Well, good for me! That's better than what I have scribbled down today. But I do think it works. This is fun, and it mixes all these emotions and tones together. It's sincere, but it's camp. You've got yearning, a faux Beatles sound, and a lot of tempo changes. It's like a mock psychedelic approach. It's heavy but it's comical. The comedy is in the juxtaposition. The whole idea of wanting to go to outer space because things are getting messy down here. The whole thing is just one big hook. You get it in your head and you must sing along, even if you feel silly about it!

KONJOYAN: I went back and listened to the Klaatu version and was almost taken aback by how faithful the Carpenters version is, which was maybe an indication that that the Klaatu song was not bad. And the call-in DJ part at the beginning of the Carpenters version shows a great sense of humor. This was one song I didn't think would hold up well, but it did. It still sounds good. And just a note on the *If I Were a Carpenter* angle on this: I think it was the latest Carpenters song that was covered on that album. I don't know about you, Matt, but I remember being surprised that this got covered on the album.

WALLACE: The fact that Babes in Toyland covered it on that album was a pretty bold move on their part. They weren't just covering a cover, this was a big, sprawling piece of music to a rock band to record. I thought it was gutsy.

Rehearsing for the German TV show *Starparade*, May 10, 1978.

Released October 13, 1978
Produced by Richard Carpenter
Associate Producer: Karen Carpenter
Recorded at A&M Studios, Hollywood, CA

Top Billboard Position: #145

RIAA Certification: Platinum

Singles:
"The Christmas Song" / "Merry Christmas, Darling"

with Michelle Berting Brett, Rob Shirakbari, and Gary Theroux

From the time they signed with A&M Records in 1969, the Carpenters expressed a desire to record a Christmas album. Holiday and seasonal music proved to be the ideal showcase for Karen's voice, but due to touring and recording schedules, she and Richard had only been able to fit in two such offerings over the years, "Merry Christmas, Darling" in 1970 and "Santa Claus Is Comin' to Town" in 1974.

In preparation for *The Carpenters at Christmas*, a TV special for ABC-TV, recording sessions commenced in August 1977, and it was quickly decided that these recordings would serve as the foundation for an entire album of Christmas music. As with *Passage*, they enlisted Peter Knight who, along with veteran arranger Billy May, brought the concept to life with the help of an eighty-piece orchestra and seventy-voice choir.

Construction of the album continued into the New Year and on and off between other sessions, tours, and television tapings. In all, the

(previous page)
On the set of their *Christmas Portrait* special for ABC-TV, October 1978.

(right)
On the set of *The Carpenters at Christmas* TV special, 1977.

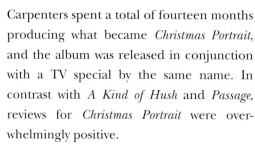

Carpenters spent a total of fourteen months producing what became *Christmas Portrait*, and the album was released in conjunction with a TV special by the same name. In contrast with *A Kind of Hush* and *Passage*, reviews for *Christmas Portrait* were overwhelmingly positive.

It was revealed many years later that Richard was suffering from a Quaalude addiction during this time period. Disguising the problem became more difficult for him due to shakiness and slurred speech. His piano playing began to suffer, and the playing of certain intricate parts was out of the question.

On December 3, Richard fumbled through the annual Winter Festival Concert with the Cal State Long Beach choir and orchestra. A week later he was bedridden, but Karen was determined to keep their scheduled promotional dates in London. She explained in television and radio interviews that Richard's absence was due to the flu and tried to dispel rumors of a possible split between the duo.

SCHMIDT: *Christmas Portrait* **opens with Richard's a cappella rendition of "O Come, O Come Emmanuel." This leads into the Overture, which was an unusual element for a pop album in 1978, but it was a dramatic and effective way to set the stage.**

SHIRAKBARI: It's striking how cinematic this album is. It's not just a collection of songs. Instead, it's as if we're experiencing a movie and the whole spirit of Christmas is being expressed through these various scenes. The Carpenters really got the feeling of Christmas right. This is the kind of record you can put on in the background of a dinner party at Christmastime and it sits in the background in a lovely way. But when you really focus on it and listen intently, all that material and substance is there, too.

BRETT: This album was a masterful construction. It's amazing how beautifully this overture transitions through the commercial and fun Christmas songs to the sacred. This is a great setup and tease, if you will, for Karen's voice to follow.

Singing "Adeste Fideles" with their guest Gene Kelly on *The Carpenters: A Christmas Portrait* TV special.

SCHMIDT: And Karen makes her entrance on "Christmas Waltz." How would you describe her arrival on the scene after all that growing anticipation?

SHIRAKBARI: There may be overtures with massive orchestras and medleys with huge choirs, but you peel all that back and there's Karen, front and center. She doesn't even make an appearance until a good five minutes into the record, but there's something brilliant about that. Most listeners would think that she would be the first thing you'd hear, but they hold that back.

THEROUX: "Christmas Waltz" is an interesting choice because it's doesn't turn up on a lot of Christmas albums. It's not one of the key standards, but it worked perfectly here. That's the important thing. And coming off the mood and tone of that opener, "Sleigh Ride" is an absolute delight. They probably figured that coming out of "Christmas Waltz" and going right into "Sleigh Ride" would be euphoric.

Let's remember what music is. Music is a way of using sound to paint portraits of human emotion. Paint has no emotion, but it can be arranged on a canvas in such a way as to create an emotional reaction in those who see it. And sound is the same thing. It can be manipulated to create portraits of different feelings. The reason anyone takes an album off the shelf is the way it makes you feel. And Richard and Karen were very much aware of the emotional impact of each of these selections.

BRETT: Karen's vocals always paint a picture. Her beautiful handling of a lyric is especially evident on "Christmas Waltz." The lush instrumental break and the quiet, restrained ending make for a magical song all around. I love "Sleigh Ride," too, and the cold opening of Karen's is flawless. The key of the song takes advantage of Karen's warm low notes and is the perfect foundation for the arrangement to build on.

SHIRAKBARI: The songs on this album all transition right into one another, like a complete story. There's a sense of connectedness, and it's obvious that a great deal of thought went into the sequencing.

THEROUX: Think about the way most Christmas albums are made. Just about every artist figures they'll add one evergreen Christmas album to their catalog at some point in their career. They round up about twelve songs, record them all separately, and then come up with some way to sequence them. *Christmas Portrait* is not just a bunch of tracks. Richard and Karen put a lot of thought and careful planning into this album.

SCHMIDT: Gary, you met and interviewed Karen and Richard in October of 1978, just a couple of weeks after this album was released. Tell us about that experience.

Karen, 1977.

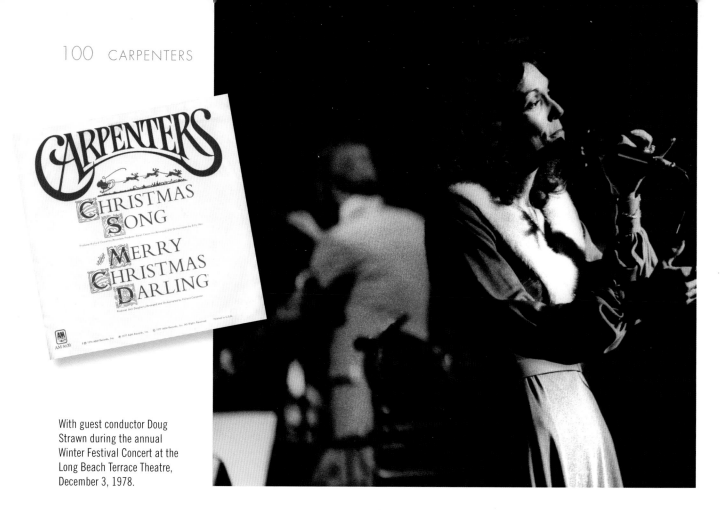

With guest conductor Doug Strawn during the annual Winter Festival Concert at the Long Beach Terrace Theatre, December 3, 1978.

THEROUX: I was thrilled when I was finally given the OK to interview them in their bungalow at A&M Records in Hollywood. Karen met me at the door with the most dazzling smile and eyes. They were just mesmerizing. She and I sat down and had our eyes locked on each other for the entire interview as Richard paced around the room. I basically had them tell me the story behind their career and their hits.

Karen loved Christmas music and was quite enthusiastic about it, and I got the impression that she and Richard had wanted to do a Christmas album for quite a long time. When they finally got the OK, the two of them jumped into this project with enormous enthusiasm. The original idea was that they would make a double album, so they recorded and recorded and spent a lot of time researching different songs.

SCHMIDT: There are three main categories of Christmas music: the traditional Christmas carols, which are usually sacred in nature, the standards from the Great American Songbook, which are the warm-hearted and sentimental or romantic tunes, and then the fantasy/novelty tunes about Santa, Frosty, Rudolph, and so on. *Christmas Portrait* has it all and in great balance, wouldn't you agree?

THEROUX: The programming and sequencing are all important. Speaking of the three different types of Christmas music, when you're sequencing those you must be really careful with what you put up against what. To go from a silly novelty song into something that is sacred just doesn't work. You must think about tempos and textures, of course, but also what the songs are about. Most Christmas radio programming

today eliminates the carols. You hear the other categories, but you don't hear "Silent Night" or "O Little Town of Bethlehem" on the radio. When the Carpenters put their album together, though, they made a point to include all three categories of Christmas music.

SHIRAKBARI: They also planned exactly how and when to use Karen's voice. Today, you would never ever take a star artist and not have that singer on the record wall to wall. On this album, however, Karen is used like the most important instrument on the record. She is incorporated delicately and with thought. There are long periods of the record that go by without her, so when she finally comes in it's special.

SCHMIDT: Let's discuss those Great American Songbook holiday standards. We think of "Have Yourself a Merry Little Christmas" as property of Judy Garland. "The Christmas Song (Chestnuts Roasting on an Open Fire)" belongs to Nat King Cole. "I'll Be Home for Christmas" and "White Christmas" both belong to Bing Crosby. But Karen had a unique ability to make them her own.

THEROUX: Herb Alpert used to say that Karen sounded like she was sitting in your lap and softly crooning into your ear. She wasn't a belter. She wasn't a Janis Joplin or a Mama Cass. Because of that, she was always mic'd very close, which made for a very intimate, personal sound. That was one of the keys to the success of the Carpenters. When one of their records came on, that intimacy was compelling. Whatever else you were doing, you'd stop and listen.

BRETT: Karen's performance of "I'll Be Home for Christmas" is gorgeous. It's emotional but never overwrought. She was an absolute master of playing that edge. These Christmas standards really underscore the skill Karen had as a vocalist. Her versions stand up with all the greats.

SHIRAKBARI: She had a tone that was so beautiful that she really could sing just about anything and you would love it. You take a beautiful song, a beautiful arrangement, a little bit of melancholy, and it becomes fresh again.

SCHMIDT: Rob, would you please speak to the work that Peter Knight and Billy May had to do to arrange, orchestrate, and bring this sort of album to life?

Arriving in rainy London on December 10, 1978 to promote *Christmas Portrait* and their new UK hits collection, *The Singles 1974-1978*.

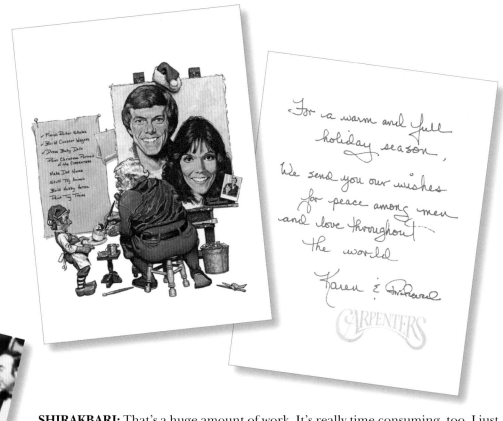

SHIRAKBARI: That's a huge amount of work. It's really time consuming, too. I just finished writing a new live show for Dionne Warwick that we premiered in Hamburg. The orchestrations were mostly of Bacharach material written for orchestra. It's a massive amount of time-consuming work to do all the orchestrating. There was most certainly some heavy lifting done by those guys. Even with the work of those very talented orchestrators, though, I still sense Richard's guidance in the building of the basic architecture.

THEROUX: Remember that it was Billy May, along with Nelson Riddle, who did so many of the great Frank Sinatra arrangements. That type of material, like "I'll Be Home for Christmas" and those other vintage compositions, that's Billy May. I can understand Richard wanting to bring him in to get that particular type of classy feel for those standards.

SCHMIDT: Let's go back to the album. Side two starts with "Jingle Bells" and then a combination of "First Snowfall" and "Let It Snow," all of which were all patterned after the Spike Jones *Xmas Spectacular* album that Karen and Richard loved so much as kids. Can you hear the influences of the Spike Jones album or any other classic holiday albums?

THEROUX: Spike Jones was certainly not the first to do what he did with his Christmas album, which was to craft it as a cohesive album-length work rather than a random bunch of individual tracks. People like Gordon Jenkins did that with *Manhattan Tower* in 1946. That was a long musical composition of selections that were segued and linked, not just a collection of tracks. It was fully produced from end to end. The Carpenters were doing that same sort of thing.

BRETT: I love the Spike Jones influence on "Jingle Bells." It gives a fresh flavor to a song that could be the same-old, same-old.

SHIRAKBARI: Richard was a big fan of the music of the 1940s and 1950s and all that material we're referencing. It's certainly evident here.

THEROUX: That's how he was familiar with Billy May's work.

SHIRAKBARI: I slightly prefer Peter Knight's work on this record over Billy's. Peter's stuff is just spectacular.

THEROUX: Peter Knight was involved with a lot of Christmas recordings over the years, including some lush orchestral stuff. He did at least one Christmas album by himself, meaning him and his orchestra, but he also backed a lot of other people.

SHIRAKBARI: There are some moments in this album where it feels very much like "This is a TV show." It had a cinematic feel in general, but there are times in the writing where it sounds like it was for a TV show.

SCHMIDT: And in some cases, it was. Songs like "Sleigh Ride," "It's Christmas Time/Sleep Well, Little Children," the "Winter Wonderland" medley, and others were arranged and recorded for their Christmas specials on ABC-TV.

THEROUX: The *Christmas Portrait* album was perhaps a reconception of their television specials. There are certain things they found would work well on television, not only audio-wise but visually, and they wanted to do a Christmas concept album. But they probably also figured that some of the stuff from TV wouldn't work well on the album. They most likely researched the kinds of songs they could build into a cohesive album-length production for audio only.

BRETT: This medley has everything: the excitement of the season in "Winter Wonderland," the magic of "Silver Bells" with so much musical fun in the instrumental feature, and the ending with all that heart and yearning in "White Christmas." This is a tip of the hat to the medley of the same songs by Spike Jones, but also the classic Christmas recordings of Bing Crosby and Perry Como.

SHIRAKBARI: Again, with the TV show, there was a bravery with putting that out there in record form and not stripping it down or thinking it had to be knocked down to just a collection of songs. To let these medleys sit, let the transitions happen, and let that whole feeling exist on record. Nobody does that anymore.

SCHMIDT: "Merry Christmas, Darling" was first released as a single in 1970. This 1978 version was basically a clone,

Karen's Century City condo at Christmas, 1978.

the main change being Karen's rerecorded lead vocal. Her voice had developed and matured since that first recording when she was just twenty years old.

SHIRAKBARI: It's one of my favorite tracks on the record and that's most definitely due to Richard's restraint in the arrangement. It's not performed in that cinematic manner. It's a break from the bombast of some of the other arrangements, and it feels like a true Carpenters song.

BRETT: I love the backstory of this song. Frank Pooler, Karen and Richard's choral director at Cal State Long Beach, wrote the lyric as a young man and passed it along to Richard, who wrote the music as a young man many years later. There was something perfect about the timing there. I don't believe Karen ever had a misstep vocally, but I completely understand her decision to rerecord the vocal. I know from listening to early recordings of my own voice that I sometimes hear the extra effort in a performance that simply wasn't needed. Perhaps Karen felt that way.

SCHMIDT: They recorded two versions of "Ave Maria," the Schubert and the Bach/Gounod, the latter chosen for inclusion here. This song is so demanding in terms of vocal range. Karen was known for her basement notes but wasn't one to ever show off in terms of her vocal abilities. Was this song a stretch for her?

THEROUX: I would think it was certainly a challenge for her because she had a small voice. But it was an extremely expressive voice. It's one of the most beautiful tracks she ever cut. I have a feeling that song was probably a longtime favorite of hers.

SHIRAKBARI: She absolutely nailed it. But I imagine it was just part of their process to say, "Let's try it." The approach was probably not, "Oh, my God, we've got to do this." Instead, it was probably "Let's just try this and see if it works." Then you do it and you go, "Wow, that's beautiful. Let's keep it."

BRETT: Karen and Richard's arrangement is gorgeous, and she gives a deeply reverent performance. It is the perfect final song for their album.

THEROUX: Her performance of "Ave Maria" is so totally believable. People go to the Juilliard School to learn technique. They get good at technique—they may even have perfect bell-like voices—but you don't necessarily believe them when they sing. With Karen, you believe every word.

REVIEWS

"They've synthesized everything to ever come out of Sunset Boulevard at Yuletide into two sides of a perfect piece of plastic. It will bring you Disney, Snow White and her snow, whiteness whiter than white, sleigh bells . . . shimmering strings, snowflakes scurrying, ring-ting-tingling, jingling and lots more besides. . . . Buy this record for instant atmosphere and have yourself a merry little Christmas."
—**James Parade,** *Record Mirror*

"There are very few weak spots in this pleasantly performed program, though it is a little annoying that the songs come one right after another with almost no break in between; you can't listen to one without getting a snippet of those before and after. That aside, *Christmas Portrait* is an asset to any Christmas collection."
—*Stereo Review*

REFLECTIONS

There was one album that I remember from the day I was born, and it was the Spike Jones Christmas album. Spike Jones was a master at zany stuff . . . but this album was a combination of nutty and serious. And we grew up with that album and just loved it to death. And when we finally got around to doing this album, which we've wanted to do for nine years, the first thing Rich said was, "We gotta do this, this, this, and this off the Spike Jones album."
—**Karen (1978)**

I enjoy doing this type of music all year round, which has been proven because it took 14 months to cut this album. While people were walking down the aisle saying, "What in heaven's name are you doing Christmas stuff in the middle of August?" It never occurred to me because I could do it any time of the day or night. Any time of the year. . . . To sing these songs is something that gives me more pleasure than I can really put into words. . . . I think we came out with 29 songs. We've got at least another 12 in the can that we couldn't stuff on the album, like "Little Altar Boy" and all sorts of them. We were dying because we couldn't stuff 'em on the record. We would have had to leave the label off! But there are so many beautiful Christmas songs . . . where do you stop?
—**Karen (1978)**

We were born in New Haven, Connecticut, and it was so nice to wake up on Christmas morning and have it be white. Fresh snowfall. There's a song on the Christmas album called "The First Snowfall" and every time I hear it I get very sentimental. . . . We remember white Christmases because it really feels more like Christmas when it's snowing.
—**Karen (1981)**

Christmastime is my favorite time of the year and I usually try and start it in November. It seems like once the 20th hits, it's kind of like a free-for-all. . . . It seems that as soon as [Thanksgiving] is over, the Christmas feeling starts creeping into your mind. I pop the Christmas album into the cassette player and it puts me right in the mood.
—**Karen (1981)**

I think the world of Portrait. It was Karen's favorite album of all our releases. Its acceptance was immediate, and its popularity continues to this day.
—**Richard (1984)**

Christmas Portrait is really Karen's first solo album, and it should have been released as such. But I don't believe A&M would have been too keen on that, especially since no conventional album had been released by us that year.
—**Richard (2004)**

We put "Merry Christmas, Darling" out between "We've Only Just Begun" and "For All We Know" in November of 1970. I'd written the melody to that song in 1966 when I was in college. Our choral director, Frank Pooler, came to me. He knew I was writing these little ditties and he said to me that he had written this song in 1946, the year I was born. He'd written the melody and the lyric, but he didn't like his melody. He said, "If I give you the lyric, would you have a go at putting a new melody to it?" I said, "Well, I'll give it my best." So at lunch hour I took the lyric into a practice room and I put together the melody. Frank was delighted with it, but it sat around for years. But then it hit me, while we were on the road in '70, that I ought to put together an arrangement of this thing and we ought to put it out as a Christmas single. It was done very quickly because we had to wait until the tour was over, get home, and then record it from scratch, sweeten it, mix it, and all of that. The whole thing was done in about a week.
—**Richard (2016)**

11 MADE IN AMERICA

Released June 9, 1981
Produced by Richard Carpenter
Recorded at A&M Studios, Hollywood, CA

Top Billboard Position: #52

Singles:
"I Believe You" / "B'wana, She No Home"
"Touch Me When We're Dancing" / "Because
We Are in Love"
"(Want You) Back in My Life Again" /
"Somebody's Been Lyin"
"Those Good Old Dreams" / "When It's Gone
(It's Just Gone)"
"Beechwood 4-5789" / "Two Sides"

with Quentin Harrison, Doug Haverty, and
Patrick Summers

After just two months of dating and another two engaged, Karen married real estate developer Tom Burris on August 31, 1980, in a star-studded ceremony at the Beverly Hills Hotel. Celebrity guests included Olivia Newton-John, Dionne Warwick, and Herb Alpert. At the bride's request, Richard and John Bettis composed "Because We Are in Love," a song that would be featured on the next Carpenters album.

Made in America was to be the comeback from a group that (apart from *Christmas Portrait*) had not released an album in four years. During that time, Richard completed a six-week program at the Menninger clinic in Topeka and Karen recorded a solo album with producer Phil Ramone (see chapter 16). For their reunion, Jerry Moss suggested they stick to their tried-and-true formula and make another traditional Carpenters album.

A year in the making, *Made in America* saw release in the summer

(previous page)
Made in America photo session
outtake, March 13, 1981.

Celebrating Disneyland's 25th
Anniversary with Mickey Mouse
and Minnie Mouse, early 1980.

of 1981 and was celebrated during a party held on the grounds of the Bel Air Hotel on June 29. By the time the duo set off on promotional tours of Europe and South America in the fall of 1981, Karen's marriage was in shambles. She and Tom soon separated, and the failure of the marriage exacerbated her mental illness and physical descent.

In January 1982, Karen admitted to family and friends she was battling anorexia nervosa and informed those closest to her that she was relocating to New York to embark on a yearlong recovery mission. Arriving at the office of psychotherapist Steven Levenkron, she weighed an alarming seventy-eight pounds. Visiting Los Angeles for two weeks in April 1982, Karen was in good spirits and even cut several tracks with Richard at A&M Studios.

Things took a turn for the worse that fall and Karen was admitted to New York's Lenox Hill Hospital. She gained thirty pounds through hyperalimentation, told everyone she was cured, and headed home in time for the Thanksgiving holiday. Back in Los Angeles, Karen shopped and socialized with friends, but those who knew her well, Richard in particular, felt she was not well.

SCHMIDT: *Made in America* **was intended to be the Carpenters' comeback album. Not counting their Christmas album, they hadn't released an album in nearly four years. What is it about this album that made you want to discuss it today?**

HARRISON: This album's a solid long player with a mix of classic and contemporary aesthetics. I find the Carpenters trying to move forward as much as trying to stand still—a dichotomous position to be sure. Due to these reasons, it has been an album I've long held an affection for and have been curious about.

SUMMERS: I'm struck by what vibrant voice she is in on *Made in America*. She sounds so beautiful and rested and her voice is so colorful and full of life. It defies the knowledge that we have in hindsight that this was a very ill woman at the time this record was made.

HAVERTY: Excitement at A&M Records was high in anticipation of this album. We had heard that they were returning to their roots and assembling a sterling, traditional Carpenters album. *Passage* had received wonderful, glowing reviews, even from some of the stauncher—and heretofore dismissive—critics. However, the praise did not produce sales.

A&M believed in it and put all their marketing and promotional strength behind it. That summer, the album's illustrative art appeared on the billboard in front of A&M, facing Sunset Boulevard. It was the full horizontal version with Karen's hair flowing back for days! It was an exciting time. The stage was set for a full-scale major label release.

SCHMIDT: This was the first album after Karen recorded a solo album and it really feels like Richard took the reins on this one. He was credited as its sole producer with no mention of Karen as coproducer or associate producer, as she had been on all of their albums beginning with *Now & Then* in 1973.

HAVERTY: I don't know that Richard so much "took the reins," but he just did what he does best: culling great songs, creating stunning arrangements, and assembling their unique aural art. I sensed that Karen was very relieved and thrilled to be back home in the studio with Richard.

SUMMERS: There's a big difference in Karen's performances when Richard is in charge. You can feel the hand of a major musician and producer at work. He knew what she did well and how to feature her voice. His arrangements never overwhelmed her voice. Instead, they provided a home for it. Richard's a musician that serves the music. That is the highest aim of any musician.

HARRISON: *Made in America* felt like a response from Richard to Phil Ramone's work on Karen's solo album as well as the changing pop landscape. He seemed to be trying to find the pulse of the period and position the Carpenters in that space as best he could.

With husband Tom Burris on their wedding day at the Beverly Hills Hotel, August 30, 1980.

Olivia Newton-John catches the bouquet.

Typical poses from the siblings, visiting their parents at home.

SCHMIDT: The album kicks off with the country-tinged "Those Good Old Dreams," which was the first Carpenter/Bettis tune on any album since *A Kind of Hush*.

HAVERTY: In music and perfume there is a thing called "the opening note," which sets a tone for what is to come. And putting "Those Good Old Dreams" in this first position was very deliberate and a wise choice. It immediately relaxes the listener, particularly devoted Carpenters fans, and says that Karen and Richard are back. This new classic set the tone for the rest of the album.

HARRISON: I agree. This is the new "classic" on the album. It has a timelessness that lifts it off this project and gives it a sort of permanence in the sense that it could be a part of any Carpenters project due to its archetypal use of melody, structure, and lyric. Those are the hallmarks of any classic Carpenters recording.

SUMMERS: "Those Good Old Dreams" reminds me of "Top of the World" and some of their earlier 1970s songs. There's a great deal of joy in those songs. Considering that many of their songs were desperately sad, I love to hear her voice on the joyous ones.

SCHMIDT: What are your thoughts on "Strength of a Woman"?

SUMMERS: I thought it was kind of the anti–Helen Reddy "I Am Woman" song. It's somewhat weak as a song and sentiment. It feels like an anti-feminist statement of some kind.

HARRISON: Despite the lyric clearly coming from an absurdly male perspective, Karen's vocal performance is solid here and projects a sort of unconscious female strength.

HAVERTY: This song is thrilling because the story is so complex and fraught with sophisticated psychological issues. Who is stronger, the woman who waits for her man to return or the woman who boots him out immediately? And Karen sings it with such grounded simplicity.

SCHMIDT: "(Want You) Back in My Life Again" sounds more 1980s than anything else they ever recorded.

HAVERTY: I don't know that it "sounds" '80s, although there may have been some musical elements that made it sound more modern than their hits from the '70s. But this is a great pop song written by great pop writers. And there was a collaboration on synthesizer programming with A&M label mate Daryl Dragon, the "Captain" of Captain & Tennille.

SUMMERS: "Back in My Life Again" sounds like a lot of the soundtracks from '80s movies. It has a post-disco sound to it. It's tastefully done. Perhaps even too tastefully done for those who liked disco. I enjoy it, but it doesn't feel like a Carpenters song.

HARRISON: This is where the record gets its lift. In many ways, this song provided Richard with the chance to respond to Phil Ramone's production abilities on Karen's solo album, which incorporated a range of early 1980s Album Oriented Rock (AOR), pop, and light post-disco formula. He also had an interest in what other pop female vocalists were doing in 1981. The successes of Olivia Newton-John and Linda Ronstadt and the emergence of Sheena Easton may have inspired Richard. "(Want You) Back in My Life Again" is arguably their grooviest offering since "B'wana She No Home" and quite possibly one of their most forward-thinking pieces to date.

SCHMIDT: Another familiar name in the credits here is Roger Nichols with "When You've Got What It Takes." This always sounded like a TV jingle.

SUMMERS: It does sound like a commercial. It's very jaunty, but Karen sounds so wonderful and so alive. For however sick she was, there was just a halo around her voice when she got in front of the mic during these sessions.

With Herb Alpert at a cocktail and dinner party honoring the Carpenters at the Hotel Bel-Air, June 29, 1981.

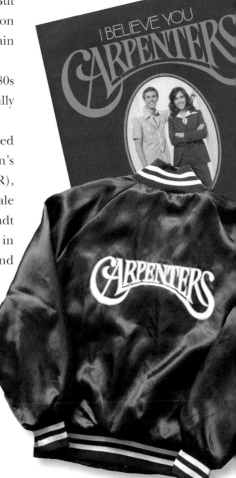

REVIEWS

"The duo returns here to the mellow MOR-pop which has brought it 18 gold singles and albums since 1970. The LP is an about-face from the duo's last studio collection, 1977's *Passage*, which flirted with rock rhythms and failed to be certified gold."
—*Billboard*

"[The Carpenters] are still singing songs as innocent and innocuous as their pleasant, pretty faces. . . . Even when disillusionment sets in, the style is so bland and cheery that you just know everything will come out all right. . . . I guess that's their appeal in these hard times."
—*Stereo Review*

REFLECTIONS

It's a very American sound—even more so, a California sound. We've been classified as a classic California sound. I have to agree with that, [and] things really aren't that different than they have been. There are a couple of things that have a little twist that I enjoy, like the Police, but nothing really that radically different. . . . Karen and I think it's the best thing we've ever done. It's the combination of production, performance, engineering and material. It's just that you grow, you hear more things, you grow in your arranging, and Karen, of course, grows in her interpretation. You just grow.
—**Richard (1981)**

We started Made in America *on June 12 and Tom asked me to marry him on 16th and I said yes on the 19th, at which point my mind kind of strayed. I always knew in my mind that when I finally got married I really wanted it to be something special. It was not only special with all of the people that came and the event, but Richard turned it into a musical event. We had Peter Knight come over and assist with the orchestrations [for "Because We Are in Love"] and also conduct a 40-voice choir, which sang live at the wedding. It was a very special day and it's a very special song for me.*
—**Karen (1981)**

From Close to You *to* Now & Then *we were having a hell of a time. We just couldn't wait to get the vocals on a record to hear what it was going to sound like. That's the way it should be. But around the time of* Horizon *we started to get tired. It took a long time to do that album and I was wearing out. This new album took even longer, but I enjoyed every minute of it. It's got to be fun.*
—**Richard (1981)**

I bought a running suit that said "Made in America" on the front. I love it, but it's a little outspoken. It's quite loud! And I wore it on Inauguration Day and I walked in the studio and Richard said, "Guys, that's it!"
—**Karen (1981)**

For some reason, people don't look at credits. Because they hear me in the foreground, they think that it's my record. I do the lead singing, but Richard does all the picking of the material, he does all of the arranging and all of the orchestrating, he conducts it, he produces it, we play it, we sing it, we take it into the mix room and right into the mastering room.
—**Karen (1981)**

We're both very big oldies fans and Richard's always made it an absolute thing to put an oldie on the album or a couple of them if we can do that. When he finally decides to, what he does is he narrows it down from 5,000,000 to maybe 100 and then he comes in with a list and rolls it across the floor.
—**Karen (1981)**

It can get to you after seven years. We really didn't ever take a vacation. We'd be on the road eight or nine months out of the year and then we'd come home and either be doing television or cutting another album. It was literally our seventh year before we took a vacation and went to Hawaii. And when we got there we didn't know what to do with ourselves. We were crazy!
—**Karen (1981)**

It's no secret . . . I had gotten addicted to prescription sleeping pills and the thing had gotten out of hand. After Christmas Portrait *was done, by the first of 1979, I had to go. I had to make up my mind myself, but I did have a lot of support. I went into a rehabilitation thing, one of those six-week numbers. It all worked out very well, but after all that it was a big change in a number of ways. You also get to spend some time thinking things over. I just wanted to take the rest of the year off. . . . But then, boy, was I ready to go in early '80. That was what became our first and last television special and then we got started on* Made in America.
—**Richard (2001)**

HARRISON: It's a pretty pop song in the Carpenters tradition, and it was clearly made to fit to Karen's singing style. It isn't remarkable but isn't a complete throwaway.

HAVERTY: "When You've Got What It Takes" is a sterling Karen Carpenter vocal and, again, shows a grounded, strong female character.

SCHMIDT: "Somebody's Been Lyin'" was written by Carole Bayer Sager and Burt Bacharach before they were married. The instrumentation was somewhat unusual for a Carpenters song. It had a very orchestral feel to it.

HARRISON: I'm of a similar mind about this entry as I am about "When You've Got What It Takes." It's a pretty pop song that isn't disposable but doesn't necessarily reinvent the wheel. The former song's uniqueness comes from its lyric, while this one pulls its spirit from the intricacy of its arrangement.

SUMMERS: It's clearly very classically inspired, and you can hear Richard's classical training throughout this piece. It's a terrific song.

HAVERTY: This is another wizened female character and an exquisite display of Karen's restraint in performance.

SCHMIDT: Let's flip to side two and "I Believe You," which was already three years old by the time it appeared on _Made in America_. They had recorded and released it as a single back in 1978.

HAVERTY: Many of us at the label were surprised to see this song included here. It had been a moderate hit in 1978, and we'd heard that Karen and Richard had recorded enough material for a double LP. If so, why was this included? I guess they just wanted it to have a home.

HARRISON: "I Believe You" is arguably the only rival to "Those Good Old Dreams" regarding its classic structure and setup. The sheer songcraft here is breathtaking. It shows that Richard and Karen really were masters of their own sort of niche in that AOR-pop realm.

SUMMERS: It's classic Carpenters and would not have been out of place on one of their records in 1972 or 1973. I liked when they stuck to their formula—not because it was familiar but because it was honest for them.

SCHMIDT: "Touch Me When We're Dancing" was their return to the Top 20 and it would be their last. There are some good songs on this album, but "Touch Me" really stands up and says, "I'm a hit."

HARRISON: We're back to something new here. Richard puts Karen in a deliciously midtempo number that

Arriving at London's Heathrow Airport from Amsterdam to promote their new album, October 21, 1981.

Performing "Touch Me When We're Dancing" on *TopPop*, a television music show in the Netherlands, October 1981.

is all at once contemporary, soulful, melodic, and adult oriented. I love the romanticism and physicality at work in the songwriting. It was a great way to pull back this sort of chaste veil that had been smothering Karen. Granted, that was what her solo album was meant to do, but "Touch Me When We're Dancing" picked up that baton and took this new Karen—and the Carpenters as an entity—into a new decade and promised big things for them.

SUMMERS: I associated this with the end of the disco era. It was a disco-meets-rock ballad like some of the slower songs in *Saturday Night Fever*.

HAVERTY: The first real single from this album showed tremendous promise. I had a press day set up with both and while we were waiting to get started, I overheard Karen speaking to a friend on the phone and she was telling them that this single was zooming up to #17 next week. We had just gotten the official word. It felt great. All the signs were good.

At this point in time, Karen looked great. She was tanned, vibrant, happy, and had been seeing a nutritionist. Before we had the first journalist come in, Karen wanted to check her makeup, clothes, and hair in the mirror. As she stood there sizing up things, she said to me, "Oh my God. Who let me out of the house looking like this? I hope the style police aren't anywhere near. Oh well, it is what it is. Let's get started."

SCHMIDT: "When It's Gone (It's Just Gone)" has grown on me over the years. What about you? Is this a favorite for anyone?

SUMMERS: This song was Richard taking back the Carpenters and saying, "This is who we are."

HAVERTY: It's the album's gorgeous signature forlorn song for which Karen is so famous. And, in the tradition of their early works, she played drums and percussion.

HARRISON: This song functions as an unapologetic ode to the sentimental and sensitive nature of love. Sonically, it pulls from that AOR, country, adult contemporary composite they had refined and made their own in many respects. It's understated, but with presence.

SCHMIDT: And, of course, they just *had* to do an oldie! And in this case, it was "Beechwood 4-5789." I know she loved it, but should Karen have hung up the poodle skirt and bobby socks by this point?

SUMMERS: There's a pretty unfortunate music video of "Beechwood." It was not a very sophisticated era for music videos in general. But if you just listen to the song, it's such a sophisticated arrangement. It's very slick. I really enjoy it and think it's a great track. It's also very American. The record is *Made in America* and it would be hard for the Carpenters to have made a record focused on America that didn't include some 1960s nostalgia.

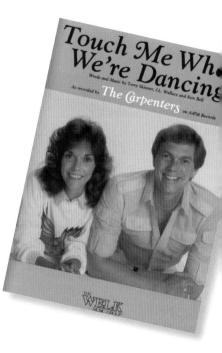

HAVERTY: For the cake to rise, it was felt there had to be an oldie-but-goodie given the Carpenters fresh spin. This song was welcomed by A&M's international affiliates and became a Top 10 hit in many countries. The Carpenters had an enthusiastic fan base around the world. Each country needed to release a single that would be the beacon to alert fans that new material was available. In many countries, "Beechwood" was that beacon.

HARRISON: Although it fared well in some international markets, "Beechwood" didn't make many waves here stateside outside of the AC charts. It's not hard to see why. On one hand, this sort of throwback pop would find favor at different points in the 1980s, but not at this point in time for the Carpenters. It was just foolish to have something so immature follow "Touch Me When We're Dancing," which was much more progressive. Sometimes, an act must make a conscious step to adapt or die, and this song did them no favors.

SCHMIDT: "Because We Are in Love (The Wedding Song)" was written by John Bettis and Richard for Karen's wedding to Tom Burris. How would you describe this song?

HARRISON: This song acts as a great bookend to *Made in America*. It wraps the album on a progressive note when compared to the standard feel of "Those Good Old Dreams" which opens the album. Peter Knight employed cinematic and classical scoring principles from the golden age of Hollywood films, which showed that Karen's voice could immerse itself in anything and come out victorious. There is, however, a tragic undercurrent to this song given that Karen's marriage imploded not long after it began.

HAVERTY: This sounds like it's right out of a Broadway show. It's almost like a musical one-act with Karen narrating and skillfully becoming the characters. In between interviews, Karen and I chatted, and I told her I was also a playwright. She was fascinated by that and admitted to me that doing a Broadway show was a dream of hers. She and Richard had a great time clowning around in their Vegas act and on their television specials. She wanted to take that to the next level.

SUMMERS: "Because We Are in Love" is the great track on this album. The singing is glorious, especially the way she subconsciously colors her voice going from childhood to adulthood. It wasn't strategic or planned out the way some lesser artist might have said, "OK, I'm going to sound like a child here." Karen just does it naturally as a response to the words. That's what great singers do.

You hear one note from Karen and it can be no one else. That's the mark of a great singer. Those qualities don't change from genre to genre. That's as true of opera singers as it is of country music singers. You hear one note from Dolly Parton and you know it's her. What drew me to the Carpenters was the sophistication of their sound and the incredible beauty of Karen's instrument. There are very few pop singers that have the kind of distinctive voice.

12 VOICE OF THE HEART

Released October 17, 1983
Produced and Arranged by Richard Carpenter
Recorded at A&M Studios, Hollywood, CA

Top Billboard Position: #46

RIAA Certification: Gold

Singles:
"Make Believe It's Your First Time" / "Look to
Your Dreams"
"Your Baby Doesn't Love You Anymore" /
"Sailing on the Tide"

with Harriet, Richard Tyler Jordan, and Mike Ragogna

February 4, 1983: Karen Carpenter collapsed in an upstairs bedroom at her parents' home in Downey. She was rushed to Downey Community Hospital, where the medical team spent twenty-eight minutes attempting to resuscitate her, but at 9:51 AM, she was pronounced dead. She was thirty-two. It was later determined that the cause of death was "emetine cardiotoxicity due to, or as a consequence of, anorexia nervosa."

Carpenters fans and curiosity seekers lined up outside Downey United Methodist Church on the morning of Tuesday, February 8, awaiting the 1:00 PM funeral service. Reverend Charles Neal told those in attendance that "Karen's story is one that has graced this world with life, with love, and with song." Later that day, her body was entombed at Forest Lawn Cypress, with a lustrous epitaph reading: A STAR ON EARTH—A STAR IN HEAVEN.

Within eight weeks of his sister's death, Richard returned to A&M Studios and started work on what would become *Voice of the Heart*, a

(previous page)
Photographed by Norman
Seeff in Hollywood, February
22, 1981.

*In
Remembrance*

She Sang
For the Hearts
Of us all
Too soon and too young
Our Karen is still,
But her echo
Will linger
Forever . . .

Memorial Services for
Karen Anne Carpenter
Born - March 2, 1950
New Haven, Connecticut
Passed Away - February 4, 1983
Downey, California
Memorial Services
UNITED METHODIST CHURCH
10801 Downey Avenue
Downey, California
Tuesday, February 8, 1983
1:00 P.M.
Officiants
Rev. Charles A. Neal
Rev. Michael E. Winstead
Organist
James Cox
Interment will be private

collection of outtakes and other previously unreleased songs, including several from Karen's last recording session in 1982. The album failed to break the US Top 40 but spent more weeks on the chart than any original Carpenters album since *Now & Then* ten years earlier. In the United Kingdom it outperformed *Passage* and *Made in America*.

Coinciding with the release of *Voice of the Heart*, the Carpenters were recognized with a star on the Hollywood Walk of Fame on October 12, 1983. "This is a very sad day and at the same time a very special and beautiful day for my family and me," Richard told the crowd gathered for the occasion. "My only regret is that Karen is not physically here to share it with us. However, I know she is very much alive in our minds and in our hearts."

Karen's funeral service
was held at Downey
United Methodist Church
on February 8, 1983.

SCHMIDT: *Voice of the Heart* **was the first of several posthumous releases of Carpenters music. Harriet, you hadn't been born yet, but I am curious to know what Richard and Mike remember about hearing the news of Karen's death.**

JORDAN: Do you want to hear the horror story of how I found out about Karen's death? Everyone who has ever known me knows that I am more than an ardent admirer of Karen's. I was working in an office at the time, and when I got back from lunch one afternoon a woman in the office, who for one reason or another always disliked me, said in a very singsong voice,

"Oh, Richard, Karen Carpenter died!" I didn't believe her. She didn't like me, so I thought it was a cruel joke. But I turned the radio on and it was true. That was one of the most devastating days of my life.

RAGOGNA: I was bummed when I heard Karen had died. But everyone in my office acted like, "Oh, well that's a shame." I was in the music business, so I was surprised that her death didn't hit them the way it did me. I was kind of on my own little island, experiencing grief over Karen's death. I left the office to get some space. I ended up at the local Sam Goody in New York, strolling around the record bins until I found the Carpenters. I was kind of mindless. It was numbing. It was shocking to me. I was in that limbo after that as I waited for the next album. *Made in America* didn't really do it for me.

SCHMIDT: Harriet, why did you choose this album to talk about?

HARRIET: I always found it quite interesting that there were only two songs that were recorded especially for this record. The others were castoffs that were pulled together to perfectly complete it. Albums are viewed quite differently now than they were back then. *Voice of the Heart* was a collection of songs, rather than an album. It was more like an amalgamation of material. For me, though, it's all about the opening track, "Now." That could have been the only song on the record and that would have almost been enough for me.

SCHMIDT: Right out of the gate, this album packs an emotional punch, doesn't it? And "Now" was a work lead recorded in Karen's last recording session in April 1982. It always struck me as Karen's message from beyond.

HARRIET: Because it was released posthumously, I think that, too. It's not like it was released before, then remastered and rereleased. The first time people were hearing this song was after she had passed.

RAGOGNA: For me, it's the exact opposite. "Now" is the grounding. It's more like now, meaning in the moment. She's singing that she's stronger, she's in the moment, and now she's ready to take on whatever's coming. *Made in America* was a good and big comeback album, but it was like she still hadn't made her statement. With this album it seemed like she was more assertive. "Now" to me was a great way to kick off the album. This is one of my favorite Carpenters albums. Posthumous or not, I felt this was a strong album.

JORDAN: I got to hear this album before it was released. A friend of mine was a friend of Karen and Richard and knew what a fan I was. He invited me over to hear a cassette tape of the album that Richard had given to him. I cried buckets. It was devastating, realizing this was the last collaboration between Karen and Richard. Except on record, her voice was gone forever.

HARRIET: You can hear that it was done in pretty much one take and you can hear that it was a *performance*. It's like you're right there next to her. There are so many of their songs with those flawless vocals of hers that were recorded repeatedly, polished

Includes:

"MAKE BELIEVE IT'S YOUR FIRST TIME"

A&M SP-4954 Printed in the U.S.A.

up, and beautifully produced to perfection. I love that this vocal of hers is so honest and raw.

RAGOGNA: Yes, I agree with you. If there's a fault in this album for me, it's the addition of the OK Chorale, that background vocal chorus that sounds like an MGM film chorus. Background vocalists could have just emulated the Carpenters approach.

SCHMIDT: Next on the album is "Sailing on the Tide," which is a mood-changer, for sure. It harkens back to the classic Carpenters sound with their overdubbed harmonies. Written by Tony Peluso and John Bettis, it reminds me a lot of "Happy" from *Horizon*. What are your thoughts?

RAGOGNA: It's a happy John Bettis song! This song emphasizes to me how some songs work best when they appear on their originally intended home. But I'm happy it was on this one.

HARRIET: It also does remind me of her delivery on some of the very early records, like "Ticket to Ride" and others where she had a throatier sound to her voice.

JORDAN: This song could have been included if they'd collected all the songs where Karen shows desire for some faraway place. Songs like "B'wana She No Home," "Boat to Sail," "Honolulu City Lights" are like "Sailing on the Tide." Perhaps even subconsciously, she and Richard were drawn to that kind of song.

RAGOGNA: It seems somewhat cliché, but most musicians live their lives through their music. In the case of the Carpenters, think about how much they recorded and were on tour. It was endless! When you're living that kind of existence, you're not having much of a life. So you live through your songs.

SCHMIDT: Let's discuss "You're Enough," one of several Carpenter/Bettis compositions on this album.

JORDAN: That's another one I thought should have been a single. I feel that "You're Enough" and "Now" are superior to "Make Believe It's Your First Time."

HARRIET: "You're Enough" always stood out for me, even before I knew that it and "Now" were recorded specifically for this album. It must have been so hard to make decisions about the singles since it was a compilation and came out after her death.

RAGOGNA: It's just more like a placeholder to me. "You're Enough" wasn't enough for me. I wanted more. I was always rooting for the Carpenters, but the addition of the OK Chorale really disturbed me. I was like, "Come on guys, you're not gonna get a hit *this* way!" I hated to see an anchor on any of their recordings. Richard was a genius and Karen had one of the best voices on the planet. I expected much more of them.

REVIEWS

"It's the duo's strongest album in a decade and contains a few cuts that rank with their all-time best. . . . The most gripping cut is 'Ordinary Fool,' a Paul Williams ballad which features the bluesiest vocal of Karen's career."
—*Billboard*

"One cannot help feel sad about the void she has left, but the songs featured on this LP are some of the best the duo has recorded in some time and the uplifting messages in their lyrics demand that *Voice of the Heart* be taken as a message of happiness and optimism. This is a fond farewell from a great singer who will be long appreciated for her inspirational and strong love for the music she sang."
—*Cashbox*

"The face on the album jacket still has the fresh, clear, big-eyed smile. The voice on the vinyl still has the sweet, slightly husky tone that completed the seduction. The only difference these days is that Karen Carpenter, owner of the voice and the face, is gone."
—**David Hinckley, *New York Daily News***

"Karen Carpenter's tragic death early last year makes this release in questionable taste even with the grieving note on the back cover by her brother Richard. Many of these tracks were recorded in the last year of her life, a time when she must have realized that she was losing her battle against herself as a victim of anorexia nervosa. I don't care who you are, you are going to listen with half an ear for indications of her physical condition."
—*Stereo Review*

REFLECTIONS

It made the time a little bit easier. I think if I'd just stayed home, it would have been that much more difficult. I felt strongly that the material shouldn't be stuck away on a shelf. Putting myself into a fan's position—if I'd never met Karen—I'd want to hear it. . . . I'd love to do another album, but obviously that's up to A&M.
—**Richard (1983)**

I wanted this album to be Karen's. I could only deal with what we already had recorded. I had thought of doing one by myself, but then I realized I shouldn't be taking any of the leads on this particular album. And even though it's the Carpenters, the vocals should all feature Karen. I know she would have wanted this. In a sense, if our positions had been reversed, she would have undoubtedly done the same.
—**Richard (1983)**

I saw Karen two weeks before she passed away. She had just come back after being in New York for about a year. She was at a hospital there and taking great care of herself. She had gained a lot of weight, she looked terrific, her attitude was upbeat, and she was excited about everything. She bounced in and she said, "Herbie, what do you think? How do I look?" And she turned around and was all excited because she thought she looked great and she was feeling good. She told me how excited she was about recording again, doing personal appearances, getting back to performing, rehearsing, etcetera. She was into living.
—**Herb Alpert (1985)**

I had the privilege of being Karen's brother and professional partner. That's the way I look at it. No matter what happens, we did have the opportunity to make those records and they will always be around. That's a great comfort to me.
—**Richard (1987)**

I just wanted to work on what we had going. It was bittersweet, to say the least, because it was all so well recorded that it sounded like she was right there in the room when you'd listen to it through the speakers. On the other hand, you knew damn well she wasn't. But it was something at the time that kept me busy.
—**Richard (2001)**

I don't want Karen to be remembered more as the singer who died from anorexia nervosa than for what she was, in fact, which was one of the best pop female singers in history. That's why, among other things I do, I try to keep the Carpenters sound alive and showcase Karen as well as I can.
—**Richard (2001)**

She came back out in April of '82 for a visit and she was so thin. She wanted to cut a couple of songs and so did I. Of course, she sounded marvelous. It didn't matter what kind of shape she was in!
—**Richard (2007)**

I lost a little sister, kind of, a friend, and also someone who gave voice to what I am. And there won't be any more Karen. Voice like that, coupled with a spirit like that, are really, really rare.
—**John Bettis (2013)**

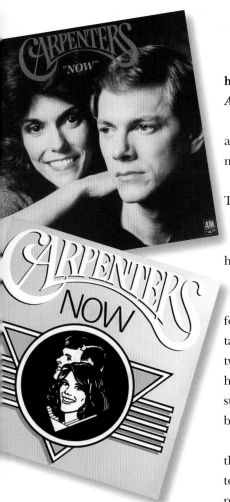

SCHMIDT: Karen recorded a version of "Make Believe It's Your First Time" during her solo album sessions, but this Carpenters recording was done during the *Made in America* sessions.

HARRIET: I think it's beautiful. She's singing "make believe it's your first time" with a real sense of innocence. Such a contrast to the solo album version, where her vocals are much rawer, sexy even. Something that always appealed to me as it's different for Karen.

RAGOGNA: The Phil Ramone–produced version of "Make Believe It's Your First Time" was about having sex. This Carpenters version was *not* about having sex.

SCHMIDT: Another *Made in America* outtake was "Two Lives." Let's discuss!

HARRIET: It's so lovely and so different. She's really pushing in this and we don't hear Karen really belting very often. There's a lot of energy and a lot of passion in this one.

SCHMIDT: Bonnie Raitt did a recording of it, too.

RAGOGNA: That was my favorite version until I heard Karen's. It had been around for a while before Karen's version appeared. The theme of this song seems to have been tailored for Karen. For her to be singing "someone said that time would ease the pain of two lives love has torn apart, but I believe whoever wrote that song never had a broken heart," that was just a perfect message. And she sang it from a place of knowing about such things. Finally. Before they were just concepts, but she really understood what a broken heart was at this point.

JORDAN: It probably wouldn't be all that important if it weren't for her voice and the power of her sound. There isn't any song that Karen ever sang that I wouldn't want to listen to over and over. This isn't my favorite song on the album, but it certainly is a powerful statement.

SCHMIDT: Side two begins with another *Made in America* outtake, a Carpenter/Bettis tune, "At the End of a Song." It has a Spanish feel to it with the marimba and guitar.

HARRIET: I love the Spanish guitar and the vibes. All of that together is refreshing. It's lovely when you hear them do something so different. There is one lyric that always sticks with me, which is when she sings, "There's nothing so hard as convincing your heart that you should start singing again." This song couldn't have had a better home than with Karen, even if it's just because of that one line.

RAGOGNA: The album *Voice of the Heart* is the voice of her heart at that moment, and my feeling is that she comes off as a stronger woman and as somebody who has finally experienced life.

SCHMIDT: "Ordinary Fool" is a Paul Williams composition from the movie *Bugsy Malone*. It was recorded during the *A Kind of Hush* sessions in 1976.

HARRIET: I love her singing this kind of jazzy stuff. It's very much like "This Masquerade." It's moody and beautiful. I wonder whether Karen had seen the movie and said, "Oh my God, Paul, I love this song. I want to record this."

RAGOGNA: I'm pretty sure it was pitched to her. They either wanted her to have the movie theme with that or at least a cover. They did have a great relationship with Paul. "Ordinary Fool" is high caliber. It was also another lost opportunity. There was a lot of overthinking sometimes, and this is one of those songs that should have been on the intended album. *A Kind of Hush* needed more songs like this.

JORDAN: Karen's having fun with this song. You can even hear a slight chuckle in her voice when she sings, "How many times have I mistaken good looks and laughs for the blues?" She's having fun. You can hear the playfulness in her voice.

SCHMIDT: Two more *Made in America* outtakes are up next, "Prime Time Love" and "Your Baby Doesn't Love You Anymore."

RAGOGNA: "Prime Time Love" was another one of those trendy recordings like "(Want You) Back in My Life Again." The jazzy middle section, however, might have been a hint of a direction they could have gone with future recordings. The Carpenters doing jazz would have opened them up to so much more material. That could have opened all sorts of doors.

With Jerry Weintraub, Herb Alpert, Mr. and Mrs. Carpenter, and Jerry Moss at the star ceremony on the Hollywood Walk of Fame, October 12, 1983.

The Carpenters' star, located at 6931 Hollywood Boulevard.

(opposite)
Karen, 1980.

JORDAN: "Your Baby Doesn't Love You Anymore" is just amazing. It's one of the strongest songs on the record with that trumpet and those strings. It's one of Richard's best arrangements and it's one of the best cuts on the album.

RAGOGNA: It reminded me right away of all their early recordings. Songs like "Hurting Each Other" and the other early classic Carpenters songs. As a songwriter, I'm always fishing for the single. When I listened to this album in 1983, "Your Baby" jumped right out at me. So what did I do? I called A&M Records and asked to speak with the A&R guy associated with the Carpenters. After I requested they release it as a single, the man quickly asserted that it was up to the label to decide what singles would be released, not people like me. That incident really offended me, but several weeks later they released it as a single!

SCHMIDT: "Look to Your Dreams" was another Carpenter/Bettis original, this one written all the way back in 1974 and finally recorded in 1978.

RAGOGNA: It's a great album closer, especially with Richard's melancholy piano outro fade. And it's the only recording on the album which seems perfect with the addition of the OK Chorale. So I guess I have to backtrack and say I like the OK Chorale, at least on this song. And the Christmas albums, of course.

HARRIET: The lyrics are about wanting to be innocent again and wanting to be a child without a care in the world. I imagine there were probably a lot of moments where Karen felt everything would be so much easier if she were just a kid again. "Fantasy's reality's childhood." It's such a lovely way of putting it.

JORDAN: Richard's ethereal piano solo at the end is just so absolutely perfect. It's so delicate and haunting. The perfect way to end the disc and the perfect way to say goodbye to Karen.

The Carpenter crypt at Forest Lawn, Cypress.

13 AN OLD-FASHIONED CHRISTMAS

Released October 1984
Produced by Richard Carpenter
Recorded at A&M Studios, Hollywood, CA; EMI
"Abbey Road" Studios, London, England

Top Billboard Position: #190

RIAA Certification: Gold

Singles:
"Little Altar Boy" / "Do You Hear What I Hear"

with Michelle Berting Brett, Rob Shirakbari, and
Gary Theroux

I t was no secret that the Carpenters over-recorded for their 1978 *Christmas Portrait* album. At one point it was even considered for release as a two-album set. The duo's enthusiasm for holiday music resulted in a number of leftover tracks, and by 1984 those outtakes and unfinished songs were a hot commodity. It was at the request of A&M Records that Richard assembled *An Old-Fashioned Christmas* by combining the existing material with new recordings.

Modeling the new album after *Portrait*, Richard arranged an a cappella opener, an overture, and a series of interludes and segues to tie one song to the next. *An Old-Fashioned Christmas* was sparse in terms of Karen's vocals. She was featured on only seven of the tracks with her voice first entering on "(There's No Place Like) Home for the Holidays," some five songs and nearly fifteen minutes into side one.

Richard recorded "It Came Upon the Midnight Clear" in A&M's Studio D, then flew to London to record the additional material with

Maestro Peter Knight and a seventy-piece orchestra at EMI's historic Abbey Road studios. A forty-eight-voice choir was added later. It was only after delivering the master that Richard was informed this costly production would be released as a midline product with no inner sleeve for notes and lyrics. And with no promotion, the album would have to sell itself.

SCHMIDT: Shortly after the release of the *Voice of the Heart* album, A&M Records came to Richard with the idea for another holiday album. There were some leftovers from *Christmas Portrait* but not quite enough for a second full-length album.

THEROUX: Yes, the Carpenters recorded so much material during the *Christmas Portrait* sessions and then they discovered they could only release a single album. They made a lot of hard decisions as to what to include on the first LP, so the second one is made up of that extra material that existed. Richard took the leftover stuff and combined it with long instrumental stretches to bring it out to album length. He had to find ways of building a new album around those tracks and find titles that didn't duplicate things on the original collection. I'm sure it was a bit of a challenge.

SCHMIDT: Let's start by discussing the material leading up to Karen's entrance, which is roughly fifteen minutes into the album. It opens with Richard's a cappella "Midnight Clear" and then leads into a big, ambitious overture.

SHIRAKBARI: There's a lot of stuff on *An Old-Fashioned Christmas* that I absolutely love! It became clear to me in "O Come O Come Emmanuel," just as with "It Came Upon a Midnight Clear" on *Christmas Portrait*, how much of a Beach Boys influence he had. Most of the time, on their records, it was the two of them blended together so I never really thought about it. Him by himself with those beautiful, tight harmonies, sounds very Brian Wilson-ish.

SCHMIDT: My favorite of all the instrumentals is Richard's "O Holy Night." It's one of the few Christmas classics I wish Karen had recorded. Your thoughts on this one?

SHIRAKBARI: It might be my imagination, but his playing on that song is so beautiful and I hear a little bit of pain in it. It almost feels like that's where Richard expresses what he's feeling about Karen. It's in that piano performance that he shows us his heart. And that little Rachmaninoff ending he does on the end, it's just brilliant.

SCHMIDT: Do you have any observations on Richard's other big numbers on this album, "My Favorite Things" and the epic *Nutcracker* medley?

SHIRAKBARI: You hear his power in "My Favorite Things." You really hear him on that one. He played loudly, and he hit that piano hard. He plays big and loud. His playing is very present, and it cuts through those records. Even though you think this is all very soft, easy, and pretty music, no, he's playing with the tone and the solidity of a piano player. And he's got massively great chops when he chooses to use them. I hear pure expression in "O Holy Night" and I hear the virtuosity in "My Favorite Things."

He has that great sense of when to use it, when to not use it, and how to build a frame around the singer and the song.

THEROUX: I always felt Richard was a fine pianist and excellent arranger, but even though he has these skills, with the loss of Karen the market for him just absolutely vanished. It must be incredibly frustrating for him. He was still a very young man when Karen passed. To have this talent but not really have a place to showcase would be very frustrating. Within the Carpenter family, you must understand the fact that Richard was the one who was considered to be the great talent. Karen was sort of thrown in there. Then, as it turned out, Karen was the one who emerged as the distinctive star. Despite Richard's instrumental and arranging abilities, there are other people who can also play the piano as well and can arrange well. The whole keystone to the Carpenters success was her voice.

SHIRAKBARI: I would also speculate that collaborating with someone else is a different process. When you're working with your sister, you've got all kinds of shorthand and ways to communicate exactly what you want and how you want to do it. That's a whole different dynamic that's developed over their lifetime. You take Karen out of the picture and put Richard in a situation of collaborating with a different artist, then he's got to communicate at a whole different level. You don't have someone there reading your mind. That can be very frustrating if you're used to working shorthand. If you're used to working quickly and ambitiously, you don't have to verbalize 80 percent of what you're trying to do. You take that to an outside collaborative process and it becomes very difficult, especially for someone who tends to be impatient, wants to work fast, and may not able to express these things very well.

THEROUX: One of the things Richard must have picked up from someone like Brian Wilson was the idea of spending incredible amounts of time perfecting a track. A lot of artists don't want to do that. "I'll come down and do a vocal," they'll say, thinking they'll do a few takes and then leave. Richard doesn't work that way.

SCHMIDT: "(There's No Place Like) Home for the Holidays," "What Are You Doing New Year's Eve?," and several songs with Karen's vocals fall into that Great American Songbook category. What made these standards such a perfect match for her voice?

BRETT: Karen's performance here is akin to "The Christmas Song" or "Have Yourself a Merry Little Christmas." It's another beautiful interpretation of a standard that stands up with any of the vocal masters.

Karen's last Christmas, 1982.

REVIEWS

"The duo's second Christmas album, following their gold *Christmas Portrait*, consists of previously unreleased tracks, save for a shimmering version of 'Santa Claus Is Comin' to Town.' Although less consistent than the earlier set, this collection features several indispensable tracks with the late Karen Carpenter singing lead, most notably a heartbreaking 'Little Altar Boy.'"
—*Billboard*

REFLECTIONS

I've always wanted to record with the orchestras in England, and I'm glad I did. . . . An Old-Fashioned Christmas is a concept album, reminiscent of Christmas Portrait and should be listened to in its entirety because one selection leads into the next. The whole album is really good and sonically is very impressive.
—Richard (1984)

There are two Carpenters Christmas albums: the one from '78 and the one from '84. And the Old-Fashioned Christmas album from '84 has the ballad version, my arrangement, of "Santa Claus Is Comin' to Town." [. . .] We wanted to get a little better sonics for the Old-Fashioned [Christmas] album so we put a little Fender Rhodes along with the Wurlitzer electric piano to get it fuller and, just for a little change of pace, we redid the sax solo.
—Richard (1985)

In one way, it's business as usual, because we spent so many years in the studio, so the mechanics of it are second nature. The troubling part, of course, is that it keeps reminding me that she's no longer here. And on the other hand, she left a marvelous legacy. In one sense it's troubling and in another it's nice to know that at least her voice is still with us. In a way, it was like working with her.
—Richard (1987)

Karen and I had gotten a bit over-enthusiastic about all the terrific Christmas songs from which to choose, and ultimately recorded too many (five to be exact) to fit on Christmas Portrait. In mid-1984, I was informed . . . A&M was interested in releasing an album that would contain these tracks.
—Richard (2009)

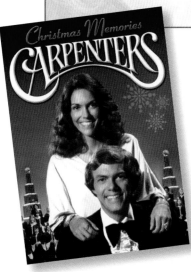

THEROUX: For any song to become a standard, there must be a significant number of people who take in the lyrics, the arrangement, the overall performance, and then say, "Yes, that's just how I feel!" It's sort of like going into a greeting card store and sorting through thousands of cards until you find one with just the right illustration on the front and the right verse inside and you say, "Yes, that's just how I feel!" Karen gravitated to the songs that matched her emotions and that's how she was able to convey them so well.

SCHMIDT: Let's talk about some of the songs in the sacred category. Richard often cites "Little Altar Boy" as one of Karen's finest performances ever.

BRETT: This song has a special curiosity for me, knowing that this was Richard's favorite performance of all the songs Karen recorded. It's mysterious and haunting, and Karen's interpretation is perfectly emotional and introspective.

THEROUX: Do you know who had the original hit with that? It was Vic Dana in 1961. It is not considered a Christmas standard on the same level as a "White Christmas" or whatever, but it's still a beautiful song that several artists have recorded over the years. It's not the easiest song to sing, but Karen nailed it.

SCHMIDT: And Gary, you were able to include "Little Altar Boy" and some of the Christmas songs on the 1997 box set you produced for *Reader's Digest*. How did you decide what to include and what was it like to work with Richard?

THEROUX: I wanted to make that set as comprehensive as possible. Since Christmas music is a key part of the Carpenters legacy, I put six tracks on the third disc. In addition to "Little Altar Boy," there was "Silent Night," "Christ Is Born," "White Christmas," "Merry Christmas, Darling," and "Ave Maria." I thought those were really the highlights.

Richard working with Carpenters music is sort of like George Lucas working with the *Star Wars* movies. Richard is an eternal tinkerer. He's never really satisfied with anything. When we put the box set together, I wanted to use the original mixes of every hit in the collection, in addition to the original album mixes of all the album tracks. "No," he insisted, "I've improved them." As a result, that box set has only a few original recordings in it. Almost every track was one of his remixes. I'm not saying that the changes were bad. I just wish he would have left all the tracks alone, fixed in their historical perspective, and not tinkered with them. He just feels a compulsion to tinker with the sound.

Richard is a very creative guy, a great arranger, and a fine musician, but he doesn't have a creative outlet anymore. When Karen died, the Carpenters career died with her. He put out a couple of solo albums that didn't really sell. It must drive him absolutely nuts that he doesn't have any other ways to express that new creativity. All he can do is tinker with these existing tracks.

SCHMIDT: "Do You Hear What I Hear?" was Karen's work lead vocal and almost didn't make it on the album. There was a lyric flub in the first verse, which explains Richard's voice at the beginning of the song.

BRETT: This is a stunning arrangement with a wonderful theatrical build. It's more amazing to know that Karen's vocal performance was a work lead. That lyric flub was a happy accident that only serves their version in the most positive way. I love the power of this arrangement as it rolls into the final verse with the choir and full orchestra, the snare and cymbal crashes. And Karen's final note is heaven!

SCHMIDT: Let's discuss their 1974 single, "Santa Claus Is Comin' to Town," which appears on this album with a new mix and new saxophone solo.

BRETT: Karen sounds so sexy and playful. It's done with such a beautiful and delicious delivery. The sax solo is spectacular as well. It's one of my favorites.

SHIRAKBARI: That smile in her voice. She had the melancholy, but there were so many of those songs where you could hear the smile in her voice. Getting a smile through a microphone, not everybody can do that.

BRETT: I just think she was a very deep person. She didn't hold back anything. She left it all in those vocal performances. She didn't do it by being a showoff. She let her interior life come through. There was a dark side, but she apparently was a whole lot of fun and had a great sense of humor. So that comes through in her vocals, too.

14

Richard Carpenter: TIME

Released October 11, 1987
Produced by Richard Carpenter
Recorded at A&M Studios, Hollywood, CA

Singles:
"Something in Your Eyes" / "Time"
"Time" / "Calling Your Name Again" (promo)

with Doug Haverty, Drew Jansen, and Daniel J. Levitin

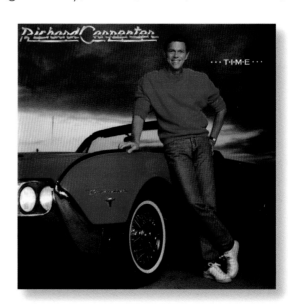

Members of the in-person Carpenters band reunited on May 19, 1984, to celebrate Richard's marriage to Mary Rudolph of Baltimore, Maryland, in a private ceremony at Downey United Methodist Church. The couple welcomed their first child, Kristi Lynn, on August 17, 1987, and the union produced four more children: Traci Tatum, born July 25, 1989; Mindi Karen, born July 7, 1992; Colin Paul, born July 20, 1994; and Taylor Mary, born December 5, 1998.

Working on and off for two years, Richard released his first solo album in 1987. Featuring his own lead vocals on six tracks and guest vocals by Dionne Warwick, Dusty Springfield, and newcomer Scott Grimes, *Time* failed to generate much interest among critics or record buyers. And with a newborn baby at home, Richard chose to forego touring to support the new release. Even so, "Something in Your Eyes" scored a Top 20 hit on the Adult Contemporary charts.

SCHMIDT: In the years following his sister's death, who was Richard Carpenter to A&M Records? How was he viewed by folks at the label? Was he taken seriously as a legitimate solo recording act?

JANSEN: I would say no. His value to A&M probably dropped precipitously. As the Carpenters recorded more and more, Richard was featured less and less as a soloist. And that was primarily by his own hand. He recognized what he had in his sister's vocals and he realized he wasn't a lead singer. He did his best with the *Time* album, but he was wise to bring along some heavy hitters to assist with the vocals.

LEVITIN: I accept that that's probably true, but I find it odd because I think of Richard as one of the great orchestrators and arrangers of our era. He was a successor to Billy May and a contemporary to Clare Fischer and Quincy Jones. Those hits that he and Karen had, in no small measure, are owing to his ability to find a song and make it a hit. It's unthinkable to have a Carpenters album without his voice in the background or without his hand in the arrangement. If I had been Alpert and Moss, I would have made him an A&R person and let him find artists to produce and arrange.

HAVERTY: As someone who was working at A&M at the time, there were two mind-sets. One was a group of people who knew the bottom line and knew what contribution the Carpenters had made and continued to make through the actual sales. And then there was another group of people who were the hip, young modernists looking for the next cutting-edge thing out there.

I don't think they would have given Richard an A&R office. Although a lot of people felt loyal and appreciative of the contributions he'd made, he was sort of looked upon as more of a historian. He was there to repackage things, look through the vaults and see what else there was in that treasure trove to put out to the world. I don't think anyone at A&M was saying, "We have a new solo album coming from Richard. What's the first single or first video going to be?"

SCHMIDT: The collective sound of _Time_ exhibits some Carpenters qualities but with some updates. Joe Osborn's bass is there, Tony Peluso's fuzz guitar, and so on. It's a very 1980s sound, though, with lots of saxophones and synthesizers, programmed drums, and that DX-7 keyboard.

LEVITIN: I was excited when the album came out because it gave me an idea of what would have happened if Richard had stayed in the business as a producer. We hear him producing other singers here, and we hear his musical tastes coming through. He's among the most gifted producers and arrangers of the last fifty years.

JANSEN: If you put 1987 into a juice extractor and squeezed it into a glass, it would sound like this album. It has all the synths, you know exactly where the sax solo's going to come in and that it's going to be drenched in reverb. It's very much a product of its era and stands up well to a lot of things that were out at the same time.

HAVERTY: The reaction at the label was that it was a very Adult Contemporary and middle-of-the-road sound, while their emphasis was on what they saw as cutting edge.

LEVITIN: And that is ironic because the label made their money from a very Adult Contemporary, middle-of-the-road Tijuana Brass and Brazil '66 catalog.

HAVERTY: They did. And then they hired a bunch of young A&R people and told them to go out and find the next big thing. That was their focus. I was working in A&M's international department, where _Time_ was a very highly anticipated release around the world. There's a huge Carpenters following in England and Japan, of course, and some of the major countries in Europe, Latin America, and even Australia. Richard and I went on a promotional tour to London. He was eagerly awaited there and did tons of press for this release in England, both TV and print.

When you look at the overall picture of everything ever released by A&M, the Carpenters releases consistently sold through, whereas other flash-in-the-pan things may have shipped a lot of units, but they had a lot of returns. That wasn't the case with the Carpenters. You would think someone would have seen the potential with this album and gone after those middle-of-the-road markets, but that was not their focus.

SCHMIDT: The album kicks off with two up-tempo songs, "Say Yeah" and "Who Do You Love?" Do you feel these set the tone for the collection?

Hollywood, 1988.

JANSEN: One of my favorite moments on the whole album is that intro to "Say Yeah" with that shimmery and massively overdubbed "Yeah" chord. The first track kicks it off well. The cowriter was Paul Janz, who was a singer and songwriter of some renown, especially in Canada. He was signed with A&M Records for a while.

HAVERTY: A lot of people were submitting songs for this album.

SCHMIDT: "Something in Your Eyes," the lead single, featured lead vocals by Dusty Springfield. So beautifully done. It was a hit on the Adult Contemporary charts, peaking at #12.

HAVERTY: I love all things Dusty, so it was a real treat to have her on the album. We thought she and Richard might do a whole album together, but she was having a lot of personal struggles with her life at that point. It was hard to wrangle her or to get her to do anything. Thankfully they got her in the studio and she did a great vocal but trying to get her to stand still for pictures or the music video was near impossible. She was never happy with the way she looked, and nothing was right, according to her. It was hard to deal with that.

JANSEN: I love the song, but the lyrics are a little convoluted and wordy. I find I must listen harder to the lyrics than I should have to.

HAVERTY: Pamela Phillips-Oland is known for that. She's a wordsmith. Her lyrics are a little tricky. We had trouble with the title, "Something in Your Eyes." Just think about that. "I'm sorry, do you need eye drops?" "What's in her eyes?" We just wanted to call it something else or find another phrase from the lyrics.

LEVITIN: Richard could have called anybody he wanted to, and they would have jumped at the chance to sing on his solo album. He called Dusty Springfield, and she owns the song. After hearing her,

I can't imagine anyone else doing it. It was a great call. The lyrics are a bit obtuse, but I can't imagine anyone but Dusty singing it now.

SCHMIDT: The a cappella tribute to Karen, "When Time Was All We Had," captured a bit of a Beach Boys sound. Then it goes into that moaning and mournful flugelhorn-piano duet by Richard and Herb Alpert before segueing into the title song. Let's discuss the ending to side one.

JANSEN: It sounds like Herb is crying when he plays that solo. The first time I heard that it shocked me. And then, thinking about what she and Richard meant to him, it got to me.

LEVITIN: I didn't make the Beach Boys connection. Instead, I heard it coming from the Singers Unlimited because of the exoticism. Those are really extended chords, thirteenths and elevenths. It's got some of the qualities of Beach Boys, certainly, but I heard it harmonically as being more firmly rooted in jazz. And Gene Puerling, the Singers Unlimited, and the Manhattan Transfer.

HAVERTY: This was a gorgeous song and one that led into the title and overall theme of the album. And it was very appropriate that Herb would play flugelhorn on it. He was always very soulful when he sang or played. Herb and his brother Dave took the Carpenters under their wings and treated them like family, more than any other artists on the label.

JANSEN: "I never will forget your face in silhouette" is a stunning lyric. That throws me every time. There're so many great silhouette shots of her. It makes you think of what it must have been like for him to look at his sister and he would have seen her in silhouette on stage every night. It's a great moment.

SCHMIDT: What about "Time" itself?

JANSEN: Again, it's very much a product of its time with the synths and the Vibra-Slap, but there are still some glorious moments. There's the piano lick that takes us back into the A section after the big John Phillips sax solo in the middle. And occasionally, Richard throws in transitions on the piano and reminds you he knows his way around the 88s.

SCHMIDT: I am going to group "Calling Your Name Again" and "I'm Still Not Over You" together. They are my favorites of the selections featuring Richard's vocals and both seem to allude to the loneliness and loss he must have been trying to deal with.

JANSEN: Before I heard the album, those were the two titles that jumped out at me. I wondered if he was going to go there, but when I heard the songs and read the lyrics I realized he wasn't. People talk about "Something in Your Eyes" and say they could hear Karen

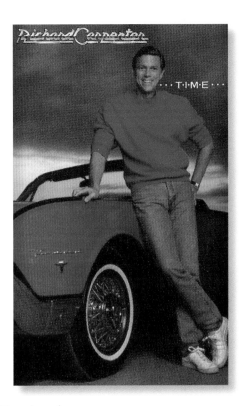

singing it, but "I'm Still Not Over You" is the one I can hear her on. It's a Carpenter/Bettis song and the way it's constructed makes it sound more like a Karen song to me.

HAVERTY: "Calling Your Name Again" was cowritten with Richard Marx. They were trying to get him into our publishing, so they decided to try this collaboration with Richard Carpenter.

SCHMIDT: "In Love Alone" was written in 1982 and intended for Karen to sing. Dionne Warwick has said it was one of the hardest things she ever did and that working with Richard was a big challenge. Do you think his level of perfection attained while working with Karen may have been hard for other vocalists to live up to?

JANSEN: I have a hard time believing that Dionne Warwick would be intimidated by anybody!

LEVITIN: She might not have been intimidated by him, but he is very particular. And he has very strong ideas. Before, he was producing his kid sister. Think about the family dynamics there. She idolized him. He was the better musician earlier in their life together and, although she had great musical instincts, she probably let him have the last word. Now, imagine Dionne Warwick comes in. And by this point she'd had a double album of her greatest hits! I can see that not going very well if Richard started telling her what to do.

SCHMIDT: Let's talk about Scott Grimes, another guest vocalist. He was a pubescent teenager, voice cracks and all. Richard and Herb Alpert coproduced his 1989 solo album, but does anyone know how this collaboration began? Was Richard mentoring Scott and sort of testing the waters by including "That's What I Believe" on this album?

LEVITIN: This was Richard working with a talented young sixteen-year-old, just around the age he and Karen were when they started gigging together. Scott had done some talent shows and such and there are videos of him singing as a kid before this record came out. He was on some people's radar, but I don't know how that got to Richard.

HAVERTY: I'm not sure how they were put together, but I know that Scott was signed to A&M around that time and had history in musical theater. They probably thought that he and Richard would be a nice pairing.

LEVITIN: I hear a lot of Richard's phrasing in the vocal. I imagine that Richard sang a scratch vocal for him, sent it home with him for a week, and then Scott came back and sang after learning from the scratch and adding a few of his own ideas.

SCHMIDT: Doug, what kind of marketing and publicity went into the promotion of this album?

HAVERTY: After an album was finished, it was circulated to the different departments for review. Then they had a marketing meeting to talk about how to develop the

With wife Mary at the
American Cinema Awards
at the Beverly Hilton Hotel,
January 12, 1991.

product, where they were going to target it, what they were going to push for, and so on. It was certainly not going to be the same thing they would do with an album by the Police. They went for the traditional middle-of-the-road, easy listening, and Adult Contemporary formats. With the first single, "Something in Your Eyes," it worked. As far as publicity goes, they sent it out to all the normal channels and it was reviewed a lot. It made a noise. We may not have heard it as loud as some of the other things that came out then, but it was properly marketed and publicized.

SCHMIDT: Was there ever talk of another Richard Carpenter solo album?

HAVERTY: When *Time* came out, I kind of felt like this was sort of a calling card for Richard as a producer of other artists. It seemed like that would be the natural progression. He could take other people and make them sound amazing, so I don't know why that didn't happen. Perhaps because this one didn't sell through well. The next topic of conversation was to do some sort of collection with whatever songs were left in the vault.

When the TV movie *The Karen Carpenter Story* was made, Richard had very mixed feelings about it. There had been lots of proposals coming in to do a movie, including all kinds of wild treatments, but he was saying no to everything. He finally decided to just do it himself and he became the executive producer. The day they were filming at A&M, I sat there next to Richard in his director's chair as he watched the two lead actors driving his car onto the lot like it was 1969. He was watching his life being recreated right in front of him, which was a tough thing, but he acted like it wasn't. He's kind of stoic. He confided to me later that it was rough, but that he wanted to make sure it was done right.

REVIEWS

"Long in preparation, Carpenter's solo album shows the same devotion to melodic craft and arrangement as his former duo's classic recordings. Vocals—strike a Beach Boys/Four Freshmen mix on 'Who Do You Love?'—may limit appeal slightly, but guest shots by Dusty Springfield and Dionne Warwick should garner swift Top 40, AC play."
—*Billboard*

"Carpenter isn't the first pop composer without much of a voice. Burt Bacharach and Marvin Hamlisch aren't going to put Michael McDonald out of business, but they don't try to. They concentrate on what they do best—and so should Carpenter. The quality of the Warwick tune in particular indicates that he should produce other pop vocalists. The title track, a moody instrumental with wide-screen scope, suggests a talent for film scoring. Carpenter should pursue these and other career directions, rather than insist on being something he isn't."
—**Paul Grein,** *Los Angeles Times*

REFLECTIONS

My intention was to get back into my music and create something new. I loved working with our older music, the Carpenter things, remixing them for CDs and all that. But I'm very much into the future too. . . . It struck home anew that Karen was no longer with us, and I found that very upsetting. Here I was, working alone when we had always been a team, working with the same engineer, the same musicians and in the same studios, and no Karen.
—Richard (1987)

Richard's wonderful to work with and we both have hearing like you wouldn't believe. We hear the same things, you know. When something was wrong, we both stopped and always stopped for the same reason. It's the first time in my life that I've ever come across anybody like that. And we always got along really well. . . . I think "Something in Your Eyes" is a really pretty song and I'm amazed it's the first single.
—Dusty Springfield, guest vocalist (1987)

We'd invited Karen to a Christmas party we were having here so we could play "In Love Alone" for her, but it was pouring pitchforks, and she didn't want to drive all the way from her apartment. I never really saw her by a piano after that where I could play it for her. She died the following February.
—Richard (1987)

"In Love Alone" was probably one of the hardest things I've ever done; listening to it is still difficult. But I'm thrilled Richard has gotten himself together and is making pretty music again.
——Dionne Warwick, guest vocalist (1987)

My lead voice is not as good as Karen's, but few are. On the other hand, I know I'm not bad. I'm just not Karen. So I went into this album and I did it and I'm happy with the way it turned out. . . . It was difficult in an emotional sense. The nuts and bolts I've done so many times that it wasn't any more difficult, or easier, than it's ever been. But it was emotionally challenging at times, without a doubt. To have to go into the studio we'd worked in for all those years, and with the people we'd worked with—which was the way I wanted it—it was kind of like, "Where's Karen?" It's something that I think about every day. And I'd come up with these songs, like "Something in Your Eyes," and I knew Karen would have loved it. Karen would have loved "Say Yeah"—it's right up her alley. She would have gone bonkers over it, I know. I just kept thinking, "My God, how much she'd enjoy making these records," and it was upsetting, very upsetting. . . . It feels good to be active and to be creating. I love to make music, so in that respect, I'm having a very good time. But there's a hurt there and it just doesn't go away.
—Richard (1988)

In this past year I've produced two A&M artists. One is an 18-year-old boy, a very talented kid named Scott Grimes. Herb Alpert signed him to the label and I produced his album, which is recently out. And I did an artist from A&M Canada named Véronique Béliveau, a French-Canadian who is very good. Those two projects just about took up my whole year because it's the same style of recording, all of the overdubbing the background vocals, the same thing.
—Richard (1989)

LOVELINES

Released October 31, 1989
Produced by Richard Carpenter
Produced by Phil Ramone (Tracks 1, 4, 7, and 11)
Recorded at A&R Recording Studios, New York, New York; A&M Studios, Hollywood, CA; and Kendun Recorders, Burbank, CA

Singles:
"Honolulu City Lights" / "I Just Fall in Love Again"
"If I Had You" / "The Uninvited Guest"

with Gina Garan, Cynthia Gibb, and Paul Steinberg

The January 1, 1989, premiere of *The Karen Carpenter Story* on CBS-TV was the catalyst for a widespread renaissance of interest in Karen's story and the music of the Carpenters. Starring Cynthia Gibb and Mitchell Anderson, as well as Louise Fletcher in the role of Agnes Carpenter, it finished in first place for the week with 41 percent of the viewership and was the highest-rated TV movie licensed by CBS in five years.

Although no soundtrack was released, *Variety* reported that sales of the Carpenters back catalog soared some 400 percent in the two weeks immediately following the broadcast. Two previously unreleased recordings debuted in the TV movie, "You're the One" and "Where Do I Go from Here." Both were included on *Lovelines*, a new Carpenters album consisting of outtakes and four recordings from Karen's solo album released in October.

The revival made its way to the United Kingdom, where the *Only Yesterday* compilation was #1 for a total of seven weeks in 1990. Four

(previous page)
1976.

years later, the twenty-fifth anniversary of the duo's signing with A&M Records saw the publication of *The Carpenters: The Untold Story*, an authorized biography by Ray Coleman, and the release of *If I Were a Carpenter*, a highly successful tribute album featuring alternative rock acts including Sonic Youth, Sheryl Crow, and the Cranberries.

SCHMIDT: *Lovelines* **is an album of outtakes released after Karen's death, and one that mixes songs from her solo album sessions with songs she recorded with Richard. Even with their disparate origins, I feel the songs flow and blend together. It's one of my favorite albums.**

GARAN: I wasn't expecting to ever hear anything new again, so when *Lovelines* came out I clung onto every single song and every note because it was a surprise for me. I don't know that I feel that it flows so well together, but I've come to love it anyway. I love each song individually. I never really listen to albums as albums anymore. I have everything shuffled now, but I'm always happy whenever these songs pop up.

STEINBERG: This was the first new Carpenters album that I remember being released during my lifetime, so I remember the thrill of walking into the record store

With Phil Ramone, producer
of the solo album.

and seeing a new Carpenters album. It's one of the few Carpenters albums that I play from start to finish, and it contains some of the best individual tracks as well.

SCHMIDT: *Lovelines* **was released about ten months after** *The Karen Carpenter Story* **aired on CBS and was the first "new" Carpenters record after the success of the TV movie. Cynthia, would you please speak to the surprising popularity of the TV movie? Did you think it would do what it did?**

GIBB: I was *so* surprised by the success of the movie. But when the role was offered to me, I wasn't even sure I should take it. At that point in Hollywood, many actors had to choose between a film career and a television career. Film actors didn't do TV. It was looked down upon and doing television could blow your chances of being considered for feature films. My agent was trying to establish me as a film actress and had pulled me off of *Fame* for that reason. When the offer to play Karen came in, Creative Artist Agency encouraged me to do it, but I wasn't sure it would be good for my career.

There were a lot of things I was uncomfortable with, most notably the wigs. They were horrible! But there was no way they could afford to buy enough proper wigs with that budget, so they were off-the-rack wigs. Some were like helmets on me. I remember sitting in the trailer one day with the hair person trying to make one of these wigs look halfway decent. The producer was annoyed that I wasn't on set and kept looking at his watch. I said, "No, I just can't. I *cannot* go on camera in this wig."

The initial script was written by Barry Morrow, who won an Oscar for *Rain Man*, so it was very good, but there were daily changes to it to make it less controversial. I was terrified of the movie coming out and being horrible because those edits watered the script down significantly. The network tried to take out anything that might reflect poorly on the family. I was living in Los Angeles at the time, but the week it aired I went to Vermont and hid at my grandparents' farm. I was terrified of it not being received well, so I was utterly shocked to find out how successful it was. I was told that it broke rating records at CBS. Except for Super Bowl events, nobody gets those kinds of numbers anymore. It was extraordinarily successful.

SCHMIDT: The title of this album comes from the Rod Temperton song "Lovelines," which was one of Karen's solo album recordings. Those solo songs were remixed in a way that gave them more of a "Carpenters" feel for this release. Paul, would you care to elaborate?

STEINBERG: It's interesting that Richard chose to open this Carpenters album with the opening track from Karen's solo album. He even named the album for this track from her solo album. But I think this version of the song "Lovelines" is in many ways better than the solo album version. He clearly beefed up the bass and

Photographed by Norman
Seeff, February 22, 1981.

brought Karen's vocals up into the forefront of the mix. Both things make the song so much better.

GARAN: I tend to prefer the earlier traditional Carpenters music, but over time I've grown to love these. It's something new and different from Karen and there's a maturity in her voice.

GIBB: My first thought hearing this song was that it's not authentic. I said to myself, "What *is* this? It's not authentic." And by "not authentic" I mean it doesn't sound like authentic or traditional Carpenters music. It makes sense to me now, knowing that it came off her solo album. They were obviously trying to give her a new identity, separate from the Carpenters as a group, but I can hear where Richard went in and put his own touches on it.

If Richard was encouraging Karen to go off and do a solo album, it must have been with hesitation. It was probably painful for him to think that she might have a career without him. When the two of them first became successful, the family considered Richard to be a prodigy. He was the music star and Karen was behind the drums. Then they realized that she could sing! They couldn't have been the Carpenters without Richard, of course, but she was the voice of the group.

SCHMIDT: "Where Do I Go from Here?" was introduced in *The Karen Carpenter Story*. It was one of several songs the Carpenters recorded in 1978 between the releases of *Passage* and *Christmas Portrait*. Most of them remained unreleased until after Karen's death.

GIBB: I didn't know any of that, but I can speak about the song. This is a quintessential Carpenters song. The harmonies, the phrasing, the way she modifies her vowels and everything about it is classic Carpenters. I figured it was one of their greatest hits.

GARAN: I love that song so much. She was so tortured in so many ways, so hearing her sing those words is heartbreaking.

STEINBERG: This is one of my favorite songs on the album. We hear somebody at the age of twenty-eight being the master of her vocal prowess. But this song is associated with her struggle and irrevocably tied to those scenes of Cynthia playing Karen in the hospital. It became almost like a music video for that song.

GIBB: It's probably more poignant to all of us in retrospect than it was when she recorded it. She wasn't a victim. She didn't think of herself as "poor me." She was a very strong woman who'd had a lot of success. She was struggling, yes. But so many of us struggle, whether it's with family issues or addictions or whatever. Many of us have struggles in our lives, but we don't think of ourselves as victims. We're not watching our lives as if it's a movie. To know what ultimately happened to her and to hear her sing that song is very powerful, for sure, but it might have meant something very different to her when she recorded it.

SCHMIDT: What great perspective. Let's continue to "The Uninvited Guest," which was one of many outtakes from the 1980 *Made in America* sessions.

GIBB: It sounds like we're talking about the other woman or the other man. But I am curious since I don't think either of them had a relationship that was that serious during that time.

STEINBERG: This is a Karen "acting" song. It's overproduced, though, so I understand why it wasn't put on *Made in America*. It's one of the weaker tracks on this album, but it's similar to what they were doing on *Made in America*. It's a very soft, contemporary rock approach that sounds like "Strength of a Woman" or "I Believe You." It's one of those victim songs, and I just don't think it's a great one.

SCHMIDT: One of the songs from Karen's solo album that was more in keeping with the Carpenters sound was "If We Try."

REVIEWS

"One listen and it's clear that no one—the closest is Gloria Estefan—has filled the void left after Karen's death in 1983. There's a good reason why some of the syrupy material was never released, but other tracks, like first single 'If I Had You,' the classic 'When I Fall in Love,' and 'Where Do I Go from Here,' instantly recall why the duo was one of the most successful of the '70s."
—*Billboard*

"The recordings—released to coincide with the 20th anniversary of the Carpenters' signing with A&M Records— suggest that Karen could work effectively outside the Carpenters' mellow pop sound and could have gone on to a thriving solo career."
—Paul Grein, *Los Angeles Times*

"Though the TV movie [*The Karen Carpenter Story*] ended with the singer's death in 1983, *Lovelines* offers the fantasy sequel: Karen lives, goes out on her own and becomes reasonably . . . hip. . . . The best of these are 'Where Do I Go From Here?' and 'You're the One,' which both reaffirm that Karen was the finest ballad singer of the 1970s. No one could fill up, and fill out, a melody or cut to the blood and guts of the ickiest love song as she could. In fact, voices like Karen Carpenter's never really go out of style; *Lovelines* reveals just a few of the avenues that would have been open to her. But sadly, the Seventies never really ended for Karen Carpenter; she died before she could shed the goody-two-shoes image that shrouded her immense talent. As such, *Lovelines* becomes her essential epitaph."
—Rob Hoerburger, *Rolling Stone*

REFLECTIONS

I'm just looking after Karen's legacy with the recordings and this TV movie that was so well received. I can't help but think of her every day. Not just from working with my music or the Carpenters music, but just things. Things like a TV show I know she would have liked. Or compact discs. It seems strange to say, but Karen died before they became so well-known and she would've loved something like that, to see the albums on CD. Just little things.
—**Richard (1989)**

Lovelines is the final album of previously unreleased Carpenters material. It's 12 selections, four from Karen's solo album, which she opted to not release in 1980, and the remaining eight are things that we recorded between the years '77 and '80.
—**Richard (1989)**

We were thinking two things: How do we make a record that doesn't sound like the Carpenters, and what could we say lyrically in these songs that has a more mature attitude? Karen was frustrated by the Goody Two-Shoes image, but she was torn. She wanted to do try new things, but then she'd turn around and say, "We're going to do another Carpenters Christmas special." I kept saying, "The (Andy) Williams family even got past that one."
—**Phil Ramone, producer (1989)**

I probably said something like, "You're just abandoning ship, just taking off and doing what you want to do." I was feeling sorry for myself. It was a combination of feeling I was being abandoned—which was anything but the case looking back on it—and thinking this was a perfect time for her to get some treatment for her disorder. So I was not happy, and I told her as much. . . . I'm human and it did cross my mind that something could come out of this and just explode at which time I would be going through a number of emotions. I'd be happy for Karen because I always felt that she should have been in the Top 5. On the other hand, being sensitive and feeling I'd done a good job for the Carpenters I would have been a little bit upset.
—**Richard (1989)**

The silence was deafening. Richard didn't say much and still hasn't. He's accepted these songs kind of like stepchildren. Karen was always the sweetheart of A&M, and Herb and Jerry reacted almost like it was their teenage daughter I was messing with.
—**Phil Ramone (1989)**

I wasn't happy with the TV movie at all. When asked about that I say, "The road to hell is paved with good intentions." I thought, "Well, if I'm involved with this, we're actually going to make it the way it really happened." And boy, was I wrong. And green. It's the worst decision I ever made.
—**Richard (2016)**

GIBB: As a vocal coach, the first thing I noticed were her vowels. If we sing correctly, diphthongs are a big no-no. Rock stars and pop stars break those rules all the time, but given Richard and Karen's classical training, they knew not to sing diphthongs. If you listen to the word "try," she sings "trah." If you pay attention to all the vowels, they're very classical. The next thing I noticed were those horns. I was surprised by them. Richard always surrounded her with strings and woodwinds, so this brass section really stood out to me.

SCHMIDT: The first of two standards on this album is "When I Fall in Love," which was recorded for one of their television specials. She was such a natural at performing songs from the Great American Songbook.

STEINBERG: "When I Fall in Love" is a masterful reading of an old standard.

GIBB: Yes, her voice is so well suited for singing these old standards. Her phrasing was incredibly legato, her pitch was just flawless, and she had a classical approach to producing her tones.

SCHMIDT: Another *Made in America* outtake is "Kiss Me the Way You Did Last Night." It's one of several from those sessions that I feel is better than some of the songs that made the final cut. Would anyone agree?

STEINBERG: Yes! "Kiss Me" is one of my favorite Carpenters songs of all time. I don't know what it is about this tune, but it feels quite cool. The title sounds like something from her solo sessions, like "Remember When Lovin' Took All Night" or "My Body Keeps Changing My Mind." There's that allusion to sexuality, but it's a bit tamer. I don't know why it wasn't included on *Made in America*. It could have been a hit single for them.

GIBB: I agree. And I love the fuzz guitar solo. It's like the one recorded on "Goodbye to Love" all those years before.

GARAN: Anything she sang that alludes to sexuality, especially this song, really appeals to me. I don't think anybody ever thought of Karen as being sexual. It was probably a major relief for her to get to sing these words and be an adult. I hear a lot more maturity in her voice, too. People saw her as a tomboy, not a sexual being, so this was probably a great release for her.

GIBB: That's an interesting point, Gina. That didn't occur to me, but what stood out to me was that the content was very different on several of these, especially those recorded in New York with Phil Ramone. By today's standards, this song is still incredibly tame and innocent, but for the Carpenters it stood out as being more sexual in content.

Mitchell Anderson and Cynthia Gibb, stars of the CBS-TV movie *The Karen Carpenter Story.*

SCHMIDT: Let's talk about "Remember When Lovin' Took All Night," the third selection here from Karen's solo album.

GIBB: It's a very different sound. That signature sound is missing and there's some risk-taking. It's a different sound from the classic compositions, and it was very apparent to me that this wasn't a Carpenters song.

SCHMIDT: "You're the One," the other song introduced in the TV movie, was recorded for *Passage*, which could have used it, but apparently it was too much like "I Just Fall in Love Again."

GARAN: It's one of my top ten songs. I discovered it during the TV movie and it's been on my top ten ever since.

GIBB: "You're the One" is very classic. It doesn't get any more Carpenters than this.

SCHMIDT: Karen and Richard heard "Honolulu City Lights" while vacationing in Hawaii in 1978. It was a popular song by local musicians Keola and Kapono Beamer. What are your thoughts on this one?

STEINBERG: This is my second favorite on the album, and it has been since I got this album when I was just eight years old. It's unlike anything they ever recorded and it's so brilliant in many ways. It sounds like you're on holiday. I've never been to Hawaii, but it sounds like I imagine Hawaii to be. This another 1978 song, a time when she sounded so brilliant. The only thing that spoils it slightly is the use of the OK Chorale. That choir approach to the background vocals just doesn't work.

GIBB: I was surprised by the country sound on this. It's not like they hadn't used country aspects before, but this one came off as a country genre song. I think of steel drums and I think of Polynesia, but I don't think of Honolulu or the Hawaiian Islands as being country.

SCHMIDT: Let's go to "Slow Dance" next. It's another from the 1978 session. The song was beautifully executed but perhaps a little juvenile. Brother-sister duo of Kristy and Jimmy McNichol released their version of the same song that same year.

GARAN: "Slow Dance" is how a lot of people perceived Karen. She was oftentimes perceived as juvenile, even toward the end of her life, so in some ways this fits with her public persona.

SCHMIDT: The version of "If I Had You" on *Lovelines* was released as a promotional single and went to #18 on the Adult Contemporary chart. It was remixed for this album. Paul, would you want to explain the tweaks Richard made to this one?

STEINBERG: Richard favored this song and gave it quite a funky remix. He beefed up the bass again. He was clearly impressed with the vocal acrobatics at the end where she did the call-and-response thing. He also reworked the ending so that it would have that shouty, cold ending.

This version is slightly better than the solo version. You can understand why it was chosen as the promo single.

GIBB: That ending is so different. Nothing like anything they'd done before. The harmonies that Richard and Karen produced together as the Carpenters were very consistent, but these harmonies are different. I'd be very interested to know what she and Phil Ramone would have done next in terms of creativity.

SCHMIDT: Bringing the album to a close is "Little Girl Blue," the other standard recorded for one of their TV specials.

GIBB: I immediately knew it was an old standard without even knowing the song. The innocence of the lyric, the orchestration, and everything about it was right out of the 1950s. I really loved it. I'm a big fan of old standards.

GARAN: It's been covered by so many people. Diana Ross, Ella Fitzgerald, and even Janis Joplin did it. Back when mixtapes were a thing, I made a mixtape with five or six interpretations of this song, but Karen's version is the best.

Photo session outtake, 1976.

16

Karen Carpenter:
KAREN CARPENTER

Released October 8, 1996 (Recorded
1979–1980)
Produced by Phil Ramone
Recorded at A&R Studios, New York, New
York; A&M Studios, Hollywood, CA; Kendun
Recorders, Burbank, CA

with Joel Samberg, Paul Steinberg, and Karen Tongson

On January 10, 1979, Richard Carpenter checked into the Menninger clinic in Topeka to begin a six-week detox program. Everyone except Karen felt it was time for her to deal with her eating disorder, but she had other plans—to record a solo album—which she detailed to Richard when she visited him two weeks later. Given the timing, he was livid and told Karen she was in no physical condition to take on such a project.

With the guidance of Herb Alpert and Jerry Moss at A&M, Karen was paired with producer Phil Ramone, whose career was thriving with such artists as Paul Simon and Billy Joel. Karen agreed to relocate to New York to record her album with some of Ramone's top studio musicians, including guitarist Russell Javors, drummer Liberty DeVitto, and others from Billy Joel's band. Richard eventually gave his blessing but asked that she promise to not do disco.

Recording commenced in May 1979 and wrapped in January of the following year, by which time Karen had spent the $100,000

(previous page)
Posing for French *Vogue*
photographer Claude Mougin
in New York, February 2, 1980.

allotted by the label and $400,000 of her own. She and Ramone selected eleven songs from more than twenty recorded to play in meetings with A&M brass. The New York playback was met with cheers and champagne toasts, but on the West Coast, Alpert, Moss, and Richard were unenthusiastic and unmoved. They felt the album was not worthy of release.

Karen's focus turned to a whirlwind romance with Tom Burris, which helped keep her mind off the rejection of her album. News of the project's shelving came on May 5, 1980, with *Billboard* reporting that Karen's shelved the album to avoid interfering with future Carpenters projects. Fans were relentless in pushing for the album's release. It took sixteen years, but *Karen Carpenter* the solo album was finally released on October 8, 1996.

SCHMIDT: What was Karen's motivation to do a solo album when Richard was incapacitated?

STEINBERG: Going off and doing a solo album at that point, just the sheer determination, was astounding. She came to London at the end of 1978 and performed on the Bruce Forsyth show without Richard. She wasn't in great shape, but she sounded amazing. Maybe she was getting a taste of just being Karen without Richard.

SAMBERG: Can you imagine the courage it must have taken to tell Richard she wanted to do it after all they'd been through together over the past eight years? As far as business and creative decisions were concerned, he had basically been running the show.

TONGSON: It was an occasion and an opportunity to present her own vision for the future of the Carpenters sound. There was an experimental spirit that brought her to New York and took her away from the context they were both so familiar with at A&M and in Los Angeles. It inspired her to explore other genres and styles of music. Maybe this was her opening gambit in imagining what the Carpenters could be or sound like in the 1980s.

SAMBERG: Yes, she may have been that far ahead in thinking about her future—not just for the next year or two, but the next decade or two—knowing that every musical act or performer has to change and grow with the tenor of the times. She knew she might have to do something completely different. Maybe movies, maybe Broadway, maybe solo albums, maybe classical. She could have just been laying the groundwork for that.

SCHMIDT: Karen didn't spend much time interviewing potential producers. Herb Alpert suggested Phil Ramone and Karen said yes, based on what she knew of his work with Barbra Streisand, Paul Simon, and Billy Joel. What are your thoughts on Phil Ramone in terms of his fitness for working with Karen Carpenter?

STEINBERG: He was adept at taking artists and working with them in transitional phases. If this was the first thing he could do with Karen, imagine a second album. She clearly needed some sort of Svengali "Richardy" character to guide her, but he didn't hold her back or dictate anything for her. He allowed her to make choices.

TONGSON: I think of this album as a draft of the sounds they were getting into and an exploration of the genres they were dabbling in. Working with Phil made sense, given that he'd worked with Paul Simon, who had also been part of a well-known duo and had established a strong solo career.

SCHMIDT: Frenda Franklin, Karen's best friend, called this album an "emancipation proclamation." What do you think she meant by that? Was it a musical emancipation? Personal?

TONGSON: It was both. Karen could only imagine the pathway to her personal emancipation as being musical to a certain extent, too. They went hand in hand. Karen exploring other sounds and other worlds is one way of imagining this as a kind of emancipation. An emancipation from so many kinds of baggage, both musical and personal.

SCHMIDT: By the time the album was released in 1996, most Carpenters fans had heard half of the songs on other releases. Were those the best selections from the solo album?

With Miss Piggy while visiting the set of *John Denver and the Muppets: A Christmas Together* at ABC-TV Studios, November 15, 1979.

Outtake from the solo album
photo sessions, 1980.

STEINBERG: The four songs on *Lovelines* were in keeping with the rest of the cuts on that album. It's odd that he chose the two he put on *From the Top*. Richard felt "Still Crazy After All These Years" was perfect and many people think it was one of the album's best tracks. But I think he put "My Body Keeps Changing My Mind" on the box set to say, "See, she should have taken my advice and not done disco."

SCHMIDT: Rod Temperton of the band Heatwave wrote "Lovelines" and "If We Try." Let's talk about those first.

SAMBERG: "Lovelines" sounds too much like a TV theme song or a musical interlude from a disaster movie! It's a little overproduced, and Karen just blends into it. It comes across as a very common recording for its time. But the special thing about Karen and about the Carpenters was that they were always *uncommon*. At the complete opposite end of the spectrum, "If We Try" is a nearly perfect recording. It's of its time, but it's also timeless.

TONGSON: "Lovelines" would be more at home on *The Love Boat* than at Studio 54 or the Trocadero Transfer in San Francisco. It sounds contrived, like an iteration of disco for people thinking about what disco was supposed to be. "If We Try" is a different beast and an indication of Temperton's range and ability.

STEINBERG: To redeem "Lovelines," slightly, as a bassist, I absolutely love that funky bass. It's prominent.

SCHMIDT: "All Because of You" was unlike anything Karen did before or after. When it was released in 1996, I heard it as an alternative rock ballad that someone like Sheryl Crow might do. But in the context of 1980, was it a country song?

A&M REC LSA

WU INFOMASTER   1-038517M174 06/23/78
ICS IPMHDLA LSA
ZCZC 01356 (4-058229E174 1615 2136571333) 06-23
TLX 691282 A&M REC LSA
TDRN LOSANGELES CA 23 415P EST   RECEIVED
KAREN CARPENTER CARE ED SULZER AND A AND M RECORDS
LOSA   JUN 23 1978

BT
DEAR KAREN I TRIED GETTING IN TOUCH. AM IN TOWN FINISHING MY FIRST
SOLO ALBUM. WOULD LOVE TO HAVE YOU ON IT. ALBUM DUE TO BE FINISHED
30TH OF JUNE.PLEASE CALL ME MONDAY 476-7616 BEST
GENE SIMMONS

NNNN
1654 EST
.
A&M REC LSA

TONGSON: It captured that Crystal Gayle or Kenny Rogers crossover country sound. It was a sound that resurfaced in the mid '90s in that Shawn Colvin singer-songwriter vibe.

STEINBERG: It's such a change from the previous track. It's the most timeless on the album because it's just Karen and acoustic guitar and almost like a folk song. There's a sort of *Reality Bites*/Lisa Loeb/grunge guitar/jangly guitar feel to it.

SCHMIDT: "If I Had You" was one of the most ambitious songs on the album and a "wow" moment for me. It still is!

SAMBERG: It's almost as good as it can get, from the perspective of trying to combine all the different elements that she and Phil were trying to incorporate into this album.

TONGSON: It's one of the tracks on the album that identifies as being part of that quiet storm sound that was mainstreaming through certain white artists at the time. It reminds me of the Cliff Richard/Olivia Newton-John duet "Suddenly." It also anticipates the early Michael Jackson sound you hear in *Off the Wall* and other numbers.

STEINBERG: I love to listen to it in the headphones now, especially the call and response ending. It needs and deserves a close listening.

SCHMIDT: I always wished that Peter Cetera and Karen Carpenter had done an actual duet. I don't know that "Making Love in the Afternoon" qualifies as one. What do you think?

SAMBERG: It could have been a successful single because of its two hooks: the Cetera angle and the repetition of the title, "Making Love in the Afternoon." Who wouldn't love that image? But in their planning and execution, they just didn't go all the way, so to speak!

STEINBERG: I was going from my Carpenters phase into my indie/grunge/rock phase when I got this album. What stood out to me was that she was singing about sex like she'd never sung about sex. She was thirty years old, she was a sexual being, and she was singing about sex!

TONGSON: I enjoy the growling, predatory saxophones. It's very '80s, but hearing it with 1996 ears, it had that kind of poppy jangle sound. Whether it's Lisa Loeb as your reference point or even some early R.E.M., it's interesting to hear her in this setting. I enjoy it more than most people, not just for the salacious fantasy of Karen singing about making love in the afternoon, but also because she's doing rock.

SCHMIDT: "Remember When Lovin' Took All Night" is right up there with "If I Had You" in terms of ambition and energy.

SAMBERG: It's sort of like a companion piece to "Lovelines." And

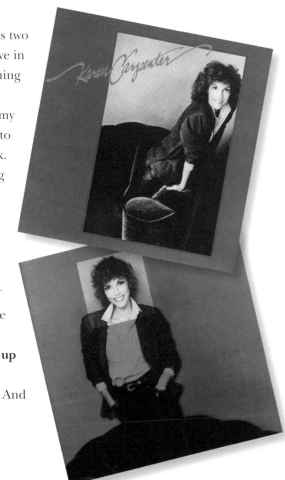

it seems to have the same problems for me. It was good for its time, but it gets stuck in that era and sounds a little more like a TV theme song. It was an interesting melody, but not necessarily a compelling one.

TONGSON: It never settles into a groove. When it gets to the part where it feels like it's supposed to groove, it gets very stilted. Rhythmically, it just feels off. You start anticipating something a little looser, like toes in the shag carpet and chardonnay in the glass, but then it just tightens up.

STEINBERG: It's such an obvious break from the Carpenters image that it feels a little too overt. With titles like "Making Love in the Afternoon" and "Remember When Lovin' Took All Night," you can see why Richard felt the album was overtly sexual, rather than just sensual. Those titles don't help counter that argument.

SCHMIDT: "Still in Love with You" is fun, but it's one of the tunes that doesn't ring true. Is she trying too hard to sound like a tough girl from New York?

TONGSON: I don't know why I'm so into '80s rock Karen, but this is her Rick Springfield track. It's charming.

SAMBERG: "I remember the first time I laid more than eyes on you" is a great line, but once you've heard it, you've heard it. It loses its eye-opening appeal.

STEINBERG: I don't agree with people who said Karen couldn't do rock. She could have done anything.

SCHMIDT: There are several disco-tinged songs on this album, but "My Body Keeps Changing My Mind" is the full-on "Do the Hustle" brand of disco. Was this in response to Richard's "don't do disco" advice?

SAMBERG: Talk about courage. And conviction!

STEINBERG: If he really did say "don't do disco," for her to go out and do the most campy, cheesy, and amazing disco song is a real flouncing of the big brother/arranger/producer advice. I sometimes call this her *disco* album, but it's actually funk, it's soul, it's blues, it's rock.

There's a very cool award-winning gay/queer DJ collective in London called Horse Meat Disco. They're an underground club that plays rare disco. These guys know and love Karen's album, particularly "My Body Keeps Changing My Mind." Most of the club-goers were born between 1980 and 1995, but when this song comes on, the crowd on the dancefloor goes wild! It shows that this song is fun, it's camp, it's disco. She was having fun and *we* have fun. And that's in a gay club in 2018.

TONGSON: It feels much less calculated than "Lovelines," even though all the disco tropes and little flourishes are there. And I love the idea of just how much it pissed Richard off!

SCHMIDT: "Make Believe It's Your First Time" was also familiar to Carpenters fans long before this album saw the light of day since a Carpenters version appeared on *Voice of the Heart* in 1983.

REVIEWS

"For anyone accustomed to hearing her virginal delivery on mope-pop standards like 'Goodbye to Love,' few things will be more disconcerting than the sound of Karen Carpenter loving to love you, baby."
—David Browne, *Entertainment Weekly*

"*Karen Carpenter* may not be the great American pop album, but it holds up with anything that like-minded singers—Streisand, Newton-John—were recording at the time, and especially with anything the Carpenters put out immediately before or after. If there is no 'We've Only Just Begun' on the album, it doesn't really matter. Fans typically crave an artist's most personal work—even if it isn't a masterpiece."
—Rob Hoerburger, *New York Times Magazine*

"Karen sounds ill at ease with a moan or a twang in her voice. That voice was a superb pop instrument. So give *Karen Carpenter* an indulgent listen, then wash the taste out of your ear with a dose of good music. The Singles 1969–1973 would be a fine antidote."
—Richard Corliss, *Time*

REFLECTIONS

We will never ever split the Carpenters because it's been too good and we enjoy it too much. But we might each try something we want to do individually. I'd like to make a movie and a solo album. I have never been able to be categorized as a female vocalist, which infuriates me. I have always wanted to win a "female vocalist award."
—**Karen (1978)**

I'm trying to take the syrup out. I tell her, "Look, you're 28 years old. One of these days your brother's going to retire and your mother won't be standing right behind you." You don't necessarily have to make a sexual statement, but you do have to make some statement of reality.
—**Phil Ramone (1979)**

Naturally I'm disappointed, but if the album had come out with her tied up in the studio and unable to play clubs and concerts, that would have defeated it. She had to deal with the possibility of one career hurting the other.
—**Phil Ramone (1980)**

It was fun cutting it and seeing that I could do all that—sing a different type of tune and work with different people. I was scared to death beforehand. I basically knew one producer, one arranger, one studio, one record company and that was it.
—**Karen (1981)**

By the time it was almost done, Richard said he wanted to go back to work. So I made the decision to shelve the solo album. It had dragged on so long that it seemed to be getting in the way of us going back to work again. If Richard hadn't decided to take time off, I never would have done the solo album. It was just something to keep me busy.
—**Karen (1981)**

I get the blame for this. People who are "anti-Richard/ pro-Karen" seem to take everything that was wrong with Karen and blame it on me. They say that I talked her out of releasing this record because I was ready to start our new album. It was sheer nonsense. All you have to do if you don't believe me is talk to Herb, talk to Jerry, or talk to Derek. . . . They believed that it didn't have any hits on it, and they weren't going to release it. It had nothing to do with me.
—**Richard (1993)**

She was one of those amazing vocal talents—and a very interesting girl, a lot deeper than a lot of people gave her credit for. She was really at a phase in her life where I think she was facing womanhood and . . . needed to expand her horizons. Like anybody who comes out of a group, it was time for her to express herself as a vocalist, and also to show that . . . maturity was setting in. The goody-two-shoes thing, I think, was getting to be a problem for her. Not on a personal level, but career-wise.
—**Phil Ramone (1996)**

Timing is important on a record release. I blame myself for some of the songs sounding a bit dated now, but it was recorded at the time of Saturday Night Fever *and all those other disco hits. When it didn't come out, I thought, "Oh, damn. This won't have a long shelf life." . . . I hope her fans will excuse some of it, but I don't apologize for any of it. I know how she felt about it, and I know how I feel. I still feel good about it.*
—**Phil Ramone (1996)**

STEINBERG: This is by far the better version of the song. Also, it doesn't have the syrupy bridge added to the *Voice of the Heart* version, which was recorded during the *Made in America* sessions. It is so intimate that it's almost out of place alongside the other genres. Perhaps it's a placeholder to remind people that, even though she could do all genres, she wasn't *not* being Karen Carpenter on this album.

TONGSON: This version is much purer in its bare settings. It was a huge hit in the Philippines, where I'm from. Carpenters had hits in the Philippines that weren't hits anywhere else in the world. "Make Believe It's Your First Time" became a standard for a lot of Filipino listeners and appears in all the karaoke catalogs.

SCHMIDT: "Guess I Just Lost My Head."

TONGSON: This is one of those songs that I group in the quiet storm category. She's finding her way around her own interpretation of that genre and it's among my favorites of all of them.

STEINBERG: Apparently, Karen rewrote the line that says "I was only trying to memorize you there." I love the idea of her working so closely with Rob Mounsey, the writer, and that they had that sort of interplay where she was able to suggest a lyric. I don't think she did that anywhere in the history of Carpenters albums.

SCHMIDT: "Still Crazy After All These Years."

TONGSON: It's a little too "on the beat" for me. The phrasing is too straight, and it makes me miss that more soulful delivery of the other songs.

STEINBERG: I know Richard loved it, but she was trying to go against the groove and try new things. It's a masterful reading in some ways, but it also loses some of the fun experimentation that I love about the rest of the album.

SAMBERG: It's just OK. Considering what the song was about, she just didn't sound really *crazy* after all those years.

SCHMIDT: "Last One Singin' the Blues" was included as a bonus track. It's fun to hear the chatter between Karen and the band. Your thoughts?

SAMBERG: "Don't forget the break!" I love that little in-studio comment. It makes you feel like you were there.

TONGSON: This is her "Hopelessly Devoted to You." It's fun and enjoyable.

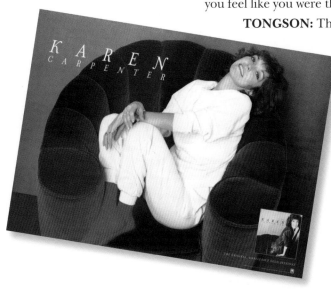

STEINBERG: This has grown on me over the years and become one of my favorite songs on the album, for the same reasons I love "All Because of You." She's just jamming with this band, no orchestration, no over-arrangement. I love that. And she sings it with a bluesy soul to her voice.

SCHMIDT: Richard told Karen that she had stolen the Carpenters sound. I always felt that, aside from Karen singing lead, the sound achieved on the solo album was quite a departure from the Carpenters sound. The approach to the arranging

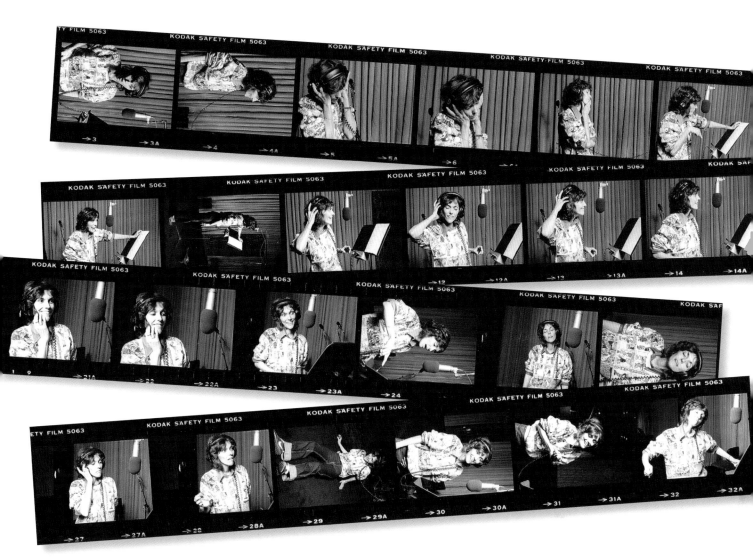

was so different. There was a brass section feel to her background vocals during the solo sessions. How do you interpret his "You've stolen the Carpenters sound" remark?

TONGSON: Richard Carpenter did not have the exclusive right to the overdubbing of Karen Carpenter's voice. These arrangements sound completely different from Carpenters arrangements. It was a silly point or claim for him to try to make.

SCHMIDT: The reaction to the album was less than enthusiastic. Richard and the powers that be at A&M Records were not kind to Karen upon hearing the project. Why the harsh response to someone in need of so much affirmation?

STEINBERG: It's impossible now to view the reaction to the album without considering what came two or three years later. Hindsight adds to that sense of an inevitable and rapid decline, and it's almost too painful to think of the rejection she endured. If she were still with us, though, that would have just been one of those annoying moments in their careers.

This album has been unfairly overlooked. Reviews from 1996 were average, some of them even mean. What the critics weren't doing then, though, is what we have just done for the last hour. It's important to look at this album in context and imagine how it would stand if released in 1980, 1996, and even today. The album merits a closer listening, even by many Carpenters fans who dismissed it. Hopefully this book can encourage people to listen with new ears.

17

Richard Carpenter:
PIANIST, ARRANGER, COMPOSER, CONDUCTOR

Released January 27, 1998
Produced by Richard Carpenter
Recorded at Capitol Studios, Hollywood, CA

Singles:
"Karen's Theme" / "Bless the Beasts and Children"

with Drew Jansen and Daniel J. Levitin

Shortly after construction of a new concert hall commenced on the campus of Cal State Long Beach, Richard stepped forward with a $1 million pledge to his alma mater. The 1,074-seat venue was in turn named the Richard and Karen Carpenter Performing Arts Center and dedicated on October 1, 1994, in a star-studded gala opening. The Carpenter Exhibit, a permanent display of awards and memorabilia, was added to the lobby several years later.

The enormous success of *22 Hits of the Carpenters*, a collection featuring "I Need to Be in Love" and "Top of the World," sparked a Carpenters revival in Japan in 1996. Two years later, the airing of a highly acclaimed PBS documentary, *Close to You: Remembering the Carpenters*, and profiles of the duo on A&E's *Biography* and VH1's *Behind the Music*, helped to fuel sales of a collection called *Love Songs*, which remained on the US charts for six months in 1998.

It was during this resurgence that Richard released his second solo

(previous page)
At Capitol Records,
October 1996.

effort, *Pianist, Arranger, Composer, Conductor.* In conjunction with the new album, he performed several shows in Southern California and toured Japan for a series of shows with orchestras. "Karen's Theme," a song crafted by Richard to underscore scenes in the 1989 TV movie *The Karen Carpenter Story,* was released as a single and received moderate play on Easy Listening radio stations.

SCHMIDT: I have heard two stories about the catalyst for this album. One says that Polydor in Japan requested an instrumental album from Richard to follow the success of the *22 Hits of the Carpenters* compilation, which was a huge seller there in 1996. The other is that you, Daniel Levitin, suggested the idea to Richard Carpenter.

LEVITIN: My recollection is that they're both true. I interviewed Richard in 1994 for an article that later appeared in *Electronic Musician.* I was talking with him about his arranging techniques in an interview for people in the business. We spent an afternoon together, sitting on the floor of the music room in his house, just listening to his records and talking about them. He would get up and play the piano every now and then.

"The average Carpenters fan doesn't realize all you have done and all you do," I told Richard. "I don't think they realize all of the different contributions you've made. They may know you're the pianist, background singer, and brother, but they don't know that you've composed some of the biggest hits, arranged and orchestrated them, or that you've conducted the ensembles. You could do more to lift the curtain on that. People should know."

His response was something like, "Well, we are really big in Japan. I can go over there and make a lot of money. The Japanese are always asking me for a new record. Even if it only gets released there, it will be worth it, financially." And I said, "Well, this could be that record."

SCHMIDT: There have been many Carpenters instrumental albums over the years. As far back at 1975, there was a Ferrante and Teicher album and a *Boston Pops Play the Carpenters* album, then in the 1990s came other instrumental albums, like the piano tribute by Richard Clayderman. I remember people referring to *Pianist, Arranger, Composer, Conductor* as Richard's elevator music album, but it was more than that. What was it that set his album apart from these other instrumentals?

JANSEN: This project focuses on quite a few of the songs written by Richard, including a number of those that weren't hits. "Eve" is a beautiful piece of music, even standing on its own without any lyrics. With songs like "Look to Your Dreams" and "Someday," this highlights his skills as a melody writer and somebody who writes damn good songs that stand on their own. It focuses on his ability. "Sandy" should be a jazz classic. The chord changes in that are just so damn delicious, especially when focusing on it as an instrumental. That's what keeps this from being elevator music. Albums of elevator music primarily feature the hits. A lot of their hits were not written by Richard, so this album puts a magnifying glass on his abilities as a composer.

In concert at the Carpenter Performing Arts Center, Long Beach, California, February 1997.

LEVITIN: When I think of elevator music, Muzak, Mantovani, Andre Kostelanetz, Paul Mauriat, and all that stuff, I think of rather expressionless performances. They're rendering the hits in a way that won't arouse any emotion in you. But here, Richard's touch on the piano is beyond superb. His use of dynamics and his timing on "Prelude" and "Yesterday Once More," it's almost like he's singing. And then when he brings in the harmonica, it's perfection. Richard has a kind of symphonic sense of form and structure.

"For All We Know" is like Karen's singing. Richard used all these pianistic flourishes with a Bach-like quality. His use of the oboe is brilliant and always has been. I also want to put in a word about bassist Joe Osborn, who is the king of entering at the upper octave of his instrument. As Richard explained to me, Joe starts out up high on the neck when he enters so that later, when the chorus or the next verse comes, he goes down to the lower octave and it sounds like the lowest note you've ever heard in your life. It's not at all elevator music. It's *elevated* music.

SCHMIDT: The first medley on the album is a nice mix of Carpenters hits. There's "Sing," "Goodbye to Love," "Rainy Days," and "Superstar," but also some of Richard's original melodies, like "Eve," "Look to Your Dreams," and "Someday."

JANSEN: Good for Richard for putting his melodies up against those of Roger Nichols and Leon Russell. He's at least on a par with them as a songwriter.

LEVITIN: And good for him for putting out the record. I'm glad he made it and had the self-confidence to put himself out there in a way he hadn't before. I can imagine that A&M Records thought this was more of a vanity project when he went to them with the idea. He probably got some resigned looks from folks there who weren't about to say no to him. He'd made them so much money and the version of the record company we know was built on him. It's a well-known story that when Supertramp first went out on the road, the head of marketing for A&M UK would say to them, "Whatever god you believe in, bow down to him before your shows and thank him for the Carpenters—because, without them, you wouldn't be here."

SCHMIDT: Let's discuss "I Need to Be in Love." I saw several of Richard's concerts in 1997 and 1998 and I remember waiting for Karen to walk out during the introduction. It sounded like the old days, but with a modern twist.

REVIEWS

"Having kept a low profile since his sister died of heart failure resulting from anorexia nervosa 15 years ago, Richard returns here with instrumental versions of Carpenters tunes. Trouble is, without Karen's voice, they sound like songs best suited to elevator travel. This CD is bound to upset the people at Muzak: Carpenter has already done their work for them."
—*People*

REFLECTIONS

They're my songs you know. I have as much right as anybody to record them, I knew as I was making it that people would be popping at me. But if I tried to spend my life pleasing everybody I'd be in a loony bin. . . . Absolutely [Karen would approve]. I can't stress strongly enough how much she would. She was my number one supporter. She would love some of the changes I've put on. She is in it in spirit without a doubt.
—**Richard (1997)**

I was asked by our affiliate in Japan, Polydor, to put it together. They asked for an album with piano, orchestra, and some vocal arranging. . . . At first, I wasn't quite certain, then I got to thinking, "Well, Burt [Bacharach] is a producer and arranger. He produced records for a number of people—Dionne, Herb Alpert—and then every year or so he put out an album where he played the same songs but reinterpreted them mostly as instruments."
—**Richard (1998)**

I didn't want this to be one of those assembly line instrumental piano albums where you hear the little rhythm section in the background and just play a little melody over the top. With my training, I wanted to approach this more in a classical mode—very little strict tempo and a lot of quasi-symphonic. It worked very well, because a lot of the songs we introduced have a lot of melodic sweep.
—**Richard (1998)**

The laymen still may not be able to tell you what the record producer does or pay much attention to arrangement, but they can sense when something is done well. The Carpenters songs had a lot of melody. And people have always liked a good melody.
—**Richard (1998)**

JANSEN: "I Need to Be in Love" and "Goodbye to Love" are probably his crowning achievements, as far as melodies go. "I Need to Be in Love" is a prime example of him taking one of his melodies and showing that, even without the lyric being there, it's just a damn fine piece of music. And what a killer to start a melody with a ninth leap.

SCHMIDT: We come now to "Sandy," which is their original 1976 recording with a piano melody in place of Karen's vocal.

JANSEN: It's the actual arrangement, like Music Minus One. I wish he would have done a completely new arrangement.

LEVITIN: I don't see it that way. The entire concept of the album was to show Richard's exquisite piano playing, and he plays this melody with great sensitivity and nuance. For me it's perfection. It's like Karen's singing.

SCHMIDT: Then there's "Time," copied and pasted from his first solo album. The rest of the album at least reinterprets their songs. Were these two just filler for filler sake?

JANSEN: It's the same track. That gave me pause. Why did he do that? He didn't need it for length, obviously. There are enough tracks on the CD.

LEVITIN: I figure that he just wanted to give this great track another shot.

SCHMIDT: The next three selections, "For All We Know," "One Love," and "Bless the Beasts and Children," follow the established pattern for this project. The tempo rubato, the instrumental solos, and so on. How do you feel about the addition of the chorus on several of these and other songs?

JANSEN: The one I like best is "One Love." Again, it's one of those underrated melodies and something from very early in their catalog. It's such a simple tune and one that's not overheard. "For All We Know" and "Bless the Beasts and the Children" both just kind of sit there on this album.

LEVITIN: I go back to the stated purpose and theme of the album, which was to display Richard's arranging skills. The chorus was his arrangement idea. It works for me because I like hearing him stretching out, trying out new ideas for songs that he could be complacent about. To me, that's the mark of true artistry.

SCHMIDT: "Flat Baroque" features Karen's original drumming from the *A Song for You* album. The new and updated solo breaks are a nice addition and help to set this one apart some from the original.

JANSEN: It's mostly new and there's that little snippet of Schubert's "Unfinished Symphony" at the beginning of his solo. But there's an urgency that's missing in this version. There was more of a drive and energy in the original, but in this one feels like he's pulling back. It's most likely because he's playing along with a prerecorded track from the *A Song for You* album. I imagine that when they recorded the original, Richard and Karen were recording their parts at the same time, which gave it that intensity.

SCHMIDT: Richard takes an over-the-top approach to "Top of the World" on this album.

JANSEN: It's one of my favorite moments on the album. The song itself is just fluff. It's very well crafted, but it's fluff. This version has an uber dramatic pianistic introduction leading into this dopey little two-step country song, which makes me laugh every time! This is Richard's sense of humor at its most visible. He takes that simple little song and glorifies it with a truly grand treatment. But where's the pedal steel?

SCHMIDT: The album closes with "We've Only Just Begun" and "Karen's Theme."

JANSEN: "We've Only Just Begun" is their signature song. This is a surprisingly restrained and tasteful production. It doesn't go overboard. And "Karen's Theme" is one of those this-guy-can-write-a-song songs. It's so beautiful and you can hear the influences of all the great composers he has credited as his inspirations.

At the 42nd Grammy Awards, February 23, 2000.

18 AS TIME GOES BY

with Daniel J. Levitin, Johnny Ray Miller, and Judy Pancoast

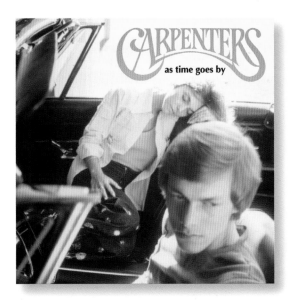

"You are the Perry Comos of today," Jerry Weintraub told the Carpenters. As Karen and Richard's manager, it was part of Weintraub's plan to secure them a deal to star in and host network television specials. He felt strongly that this was a way to promote longevity and permanence in their careers. But Karen and Richard were not so sure. Their 1971 summer series *Make Your Own Kind of Music* had been a monumental disaster, due in part to their lack of control over the sketch comedy material.

Weintraub negotiated a deal with ABC-TV in which Karen and Richard were promised full control of all future productions. *The Carpenters' Very First Television Special* aired December 8, 1976, with guest stars John Denver and Victor Borge. It came in at #6 in the Nielsen ratings that week, which led to an offer for more specials: *The Carpenters at Christmas* in 1977, *Space Encounters* and *Christmas Portrait* in 1978, and *Music, Music, Music* in 1980.

(previous page)
Photo session with Ed Caraeff, late 1974.

The music on *As Time Goes By* falls into one of several categories: songs recorded for their five TV specials, early demos recorded in Joe Osborn's garage studio, and outtakes from Carpenters recording sessions. Other assorted and rare material of this nature appeared on *From the Top*, a four-CD box set released in 1991 and *Interpretations: A 25th Anniversary Celebration*, which was released in 1994 and included "Tryin' to Get the Feeling Again," a long-lost outtake from the *Horizon* album sessions.

SCHMIDT: This is a unique album in that it's a collection of songs spanning the years 1967 to 1980 and encompassing many styles. For organizational purposes, we are going to abandon the track sequence and instead group the related songs together. Daniel, would you speak about the musical variety shows that were so popular in the 1960s and 1970s and how the Carpenters made their way into this world?

LEVITIN: I grew up in an era of television when multitalented singers with mass appeal and good personalities were offered TV variety shows. This was the norm. I grew up with Glen Campbell, Tom Jones, Andy Williams, Engelbert Humperdinck, Neil Sedaka, and John Denver. These classic variety shows had a mixture of singing and dancing and the hosts would perform light comedy skits.

In the case of the Carpenters skits, they were kind of goofy. I adore them, but they didn't have the kind of comedic sense like Jackie Gleason or Carol Burnett. It was more like the goofy kid next door, but I found it endearing. It reminded me of the Beatles. They had such serious songs, but in those Beatles cartoons they were kind of screwups.

MILLER: *The Carol Burnett Show* was the example of the perfect variety show and all of those variety shows in the 1970s attempted to do what they were doing. But the thing that was missing with all of them was the ability to really act and do comedy. Karen seemed to have it in her, and there are moments in the specials where you can see that she could really be funny if she'd just had a little bit of coaching. Richard just seemed scared to death. He always uses that word "shtick." He didn't like the shtick, but once you cut loose and learn how to do it, the shtick is really fun.

LEVITIN: I agree. I didn't know Karen, but I know Richard. He's somewhat formal. The "cut loose" isn't there. To his credit, though, I've seen Paul McCartney many times and in back-to-back performances and he'll make the same mistakes on purpose and use the same joke to recover. A McCartney concert, with or without Wings, is very tightly scripted, right down to casual asides or tapping the guitarist on the shoulder or whatever.

SCHMIDT: Let's begin with the songs from the television specials. Karen really reimagined and reinterpreted "Superstar" and "Rainy Days and Mondays" on their first television special in 1976.

MILLER: You get a taste of her doing those classic songs in a different way than we're used to hearing. Every which way Karen sang them, she always owned them.

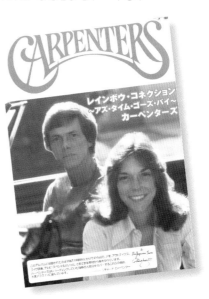

PANCOAST: These are two of my favorite Carpenters songs, but I like the originals better. This version is a little bit more affected. She was using more of her established vocal tricks by that time. Of course she always sounded terrific, but I prefer the less-polished Karen.

SCHMIDT: The 1978 *Space Encounters* special produced a slick cover of "Dancing in the Streets."

PANCOAST: This version is exactly the same as the one by Martha and the Vandellas. I love it and would listen to that over and over again, but it's the Carpenters doing the oldies thing again, just like the oldies medley on *Now & Then* or "Please Mr. Postman" or "A Kind of Hush." It's nice to have it included here, but I wish that they had been creating more current pop hits instead of resurrecting oldies at that point in their career.

LEVITIN: This comes from Richard's conception of how to have the career that he wanted, which was to have the career of Ella Fitzgerald or Perry Como. But as a duo. They were going to spend their career doing oldies and standards and an occasional new song. They were going to write their own material every now and then, but they were mainly going to be interpreters.

SCHMIDT: Most songs on this album came from the 1980 *Music, Music, Music* TV special. Their recording of "Without a Song" makes me wonder if they might have found success in the world of vocal jazz.

LEVITIN: Oh, for sure. It's a Singers Unlimited/Gene Puerling kind of arrangement. It's lush and it's got those exotic chords that you don't hear in pop music. It was way beyond what Perry Como was doing, and it was a great sound for them. The problem with that kind of music, though, is that while it's very highly regarded by critics and listeners, it doesn't sell well.

The Carpenters were proud of the fact that they brought in so much money that A&M was able to expand its roster. The Police, Supertramp, and Joan Armatrading were signed only because A&M Records was rolling in Carpenters money. Also, when you get that big it's no longer just about you. You've got a bunch of people whose livelihoods depend on you. You're an employer. There's a lot of pressure.

MILLER: "Without a Song" is another one of those songs on this album that represents something that could have been. I love that this album couldn't be over-perfected and there was no way for it to represent just one sound or style. Using all the demos and outtakes and songs from TV shows meant abandoning the perfection thing. The album is so reflective of their entire career.

SCHMIDT: Daniel, I seem to recall you saying that this was like a single-disc Carpenters boxed set.

LEVITIN: That's how Richard saw it. And this album was driven by the insatiable market for all things Carpenters in Japan. Their Japanese label asked him to go through the archives and put this together.

With special guests Ella Fitzgerald and John Davidson on the 1980 *Music, Music, Music* special.

SCHMIDT: The "Karen/Ella Medley" is the highlight of this collection, just as it was the highlight of that 1980 TV special. There's just something fascinating about Karen trading verses of standards with "First Lady of Song" Ella Fitzgerald.

LEVITIN: I also think about it in terms of the public image of Karen singing with Ella. Is Ella passing a torch of some kind? Not exactly. But Ella is effectively endorsing her, just as when Tony Bennett sang with Lady Gaga, or when Louis Armstrong appeared with Herb Alpert. It's a way of providing an affirmation that says, "This person is in my league."

SCHMIDT: Absolutely. Let's talk about "I Got Rhythm." This was somewhat of an updated version of Karen's drum spectacular from their live show.

MILLER: Doing George Gershwin is impressive. And it goes with their theme of songs about music.

PANCOAST: And there's the whole drumming theme with "I Got Rhythm." It belongs on here, I suppose, but I skip it. Watching it's one thing, but for listening it's not my favorite. I feel the same about "Dizzy Fingers."

MILLER: I like "Dizzy Fingers" because it's a taste of who Richard was and what he liked to do. I can feel the liveliness and theatricality to it.

SCHMIDT: What about "You're Just in Love," which is somewhat of an odd duet between Karen and Richard.

PANCOAST: Someone explained to me that, in the musical, it's not a love song between two people, but an older person giving advice to a younger person. I guess that's how Richard looked at it. But on the *Music, Music, Music* special, Karen and John Davidson were singing it as a love song to each other. They had chemistry. Having established it as a love song on the special, it comes across as kind of cringeworthy when you replace John's vocal with Richard's. I love Richard's voice, but I just don't think this works with him. I don't understand why he didn't just keep Davidson's vocals.

SCHMIDT: Several years before hosting their own TV specials, Karen and Richard guested on Perry Como's 1974 Christmas TV special. The medley here is longer than the one that aired. It was pared down due to time constraints.

PANCOAST: I'm not a Perry Como fan, but I like hearing Karen sing his songs. It makes me want to hear Karen sing complete versions of "And I Love You So" and the others.

MILLER: It's a joy listening to her sing "It's Impossible." There's that clear, relatable, and rich delivery and it's just like she's talking to you in your living room. That's how I've always felt about Karen. It's a difficult quality for vocalists to communicate in a way that makes you feel as though they're singing only to you.

SCHMIDT: Let's go back in time now to the demos recorded in 1967–1968, starting with "Nowhere Man," a ballad version of the Beatles song. The treatment was similar to that given to "Ticket to Ride" on *Offering* in 1969.

MILLER: *The Singles 1969–1973* was the very first album I ever owned, so when I heard the Beatles doing "Ticket to Ride," I had already heard Karen Carpenter sing it a million times. I asked my mother, "Why are the Beatles trying to imitate the Carpenters?" and told her, "It just doesn't work!" She just laughed. It's amazing that Karen could take these songs by the Beatles and the Mamas and the Papas and really make them her own.

PANCOAST: I prefer "Ticket to Ride" over "Nowhere Man," but I do like hearing this young girl who hasn't become a superstar yet. You can hear the choir singer in her, too, especially when she makes that octave leap in "California Dreamin'." It's all just so pure. And speaking of "California Dreamin'," it's fantastic. She is rocking it!

MILLER: It's my favorite song on this album. When I heard it for the first time, I got chills when she jumped up from that lower register. Then you hear those drum beats leading into that burst of rock and roll. All I could think was "My God, she could rock!"

PANCOAST: Again, it shows the promise of what could have been.

MILLER: This whole album is packed full of "what could have beens" for me.

SCHMIDT: Let's discuss the outtakes next. "Leave Yesterday Behind" and "The Rainbow Connection."

PANCOAST: "Leave Yesterday Behind" is a good performance, but it's a nothing song. I'm glad they didn't release it. It was by the same guy that wrote "For All We Know," but there's no hook to the melody. It's just all the same. It's a nothing song. I know Richard included it here because everybody wants to hear everything that Karen ever recorded, but the song itself is just not very good.

As far as "Rainbow Connection" is concerned, it's an interesting tune, but it could have been even more beautiful with a little less orchestration. And Richard treated it as a children's song. If you listen, it's not really a children's song. It's a universal sentiment.

MILLER: I hear the purity of her voice and all this youthful innocence and her singing about happiness and hope.

LEVITIN: She was able to invoke and tap into a combination of naïveté and world weariness. It's remarkable.

SCHMIDT: The "Hits Medley '76" was the finale for the Carpenters' first TV special and it closes out this album. It's quite impressive to hear them go through seven or eight of their biggest hits in as many minutes.

PANCOAST: There are three facets to this album. First, it demonstrates the promise of Karen and Richard to be pop music superstars. Then there's the fulfillment of the promise in this medley, which has all the big hits that put them on the map. They're

wonderful songs and I could listen to them repeatedly. But sadly, I feel that this album also demonstrates where things went awry with their career.

LEVITIN: I'm curious what you think went awry with their career?

PANCOAST: I don't think that they weathered the musical changes in the pop music landscape as the decades crossed over. Richard turned to these classics from the Great American Songbook. Linda Ronstadt did the same thing to great effect several years later, but it was a one-off. And you didn't see Olivia Newton-John doing that. She continued to play music that the popular music audiences wanted to hear. I think the Carpenters could have continued making viable pop hits for at least another decade.

MILLER: If she were still with us and they were still making records, there would have come a better time down the road for them to have recorded the American

A Kind of Hush photo session outtake, February 18, 1976.

REVIEWS

"Unlike the usual hits packages, this slimmer set features an early recording of 'Nowhere Man' from 1967, TV soundtrack specials and two songs, 'And When He Smiles' and 'Leave Yesterday Behind,' that stand scrutiny with her best performances. Chuck in duets with Perry Como and Ella Fitzgerald (the latter conducted by Nelson Riddle), a sprinkling of Richard Carpenter piano arrangements and the net result is an artifact that transcends the normal medley collections."
—*Uncut*

"Apart from the pretty take on the Wildweeds' country-rock-influenced 'And When He Smiles,' a song that should have been a hit for them if they had officially released it, the best of the lot is the duet on a medley of standards by Karen Carpenter and Ella Fitzgerald from 1980. While Ella is near the end of the road vocally, it is interesting to have two of the most precise singers ever trading verse back and forth."
—Tim Sendra, *AllMusic*

REFLECTIONS

When we first did TV early in our careers, it was a mistake. We were just violently mishandled. Our TV exposure was disastrous. We realized it immediately and shied away from television. We stayed away from television for quite a few years until we signed with Jerry Weintraub, at which point he got us our own shows. That's really what we needed. We needed to have full control of what we wanted to put and present on television. Since we signed with Jerry, we've just finished our fourth TV special, all four for ABC, and each one has gotten better because you grow.
—Karen (1978)

I wish I could have been in a Busby Berkeley flick. When you get a chance, every now and then on a Saturday afternoon, you'll see all these terrific musicals. That makes me cry. I think, "Why did I miss that?" Everybody's tap dancing. They just don't do things like that anymore. It's a shame!
—Karen (1981)

"Rainbow Connection," if it has a whole lead, Karen would come down and get me. . . . "Dizzy Fingers" is an instrumental. . . . It was for Music, Music, Music. *I start at one piano and I go to toy piano, I go to a harpsichord, I jump from here to there. It's really neat, but to watch. For some people to listen to, but it's an instrumental. I don't think most people are going to care about it. . . . "Leave Yesterday Behind" we will put on a future album. It's written by Fred Carlin. He was trying to duplicate "For All We Know." It's pleasant but it's not "For All We Know." But it does have a nice lead on it, so we'll use that.*
—Richard (1996)

We were a bit incensed because everyone else of our caliber was headlining at least one prime time network television special. We didn't have one. For years I'd look at these specials of other people and for the most part I don't like
'em! . . . Music, Music, Music, *now that was more what I had in mind. Now, of course, the network hated it. It had no skits—I hate skits—it was all music. The network did not like it at all. In fact, the word that came back to us was, "What the hell do they think this is, a goddamn PBS special?"*
—Richard (2001)

I saw Karen after I won the Oscar for A Star Is Born. *She was really sweet about that and also said that "Evergreen" was a great song. Then the same thing happened with The Muppet Movie. They loved the songs from that movie and wanted to record "Rainbow Connection." Richard wanted me to change some of it, but this song was nominated for an Academy Award! The song is written in Kermit's speaking rhythm, and I wouldn't change it. It was written for Kermit; it should be recorded the way that Kermit recorded it.*
—Paul Williams (2002)

Mentally, I wasn't in the mood to be doing these things, once we finally got one, and secondly, I didn't want anything with skits. I didn't want canned laughter. I hate that. Karen, on the other hand, just loved all of this stuff, so she took to them. By this point in time, when it came to the specials, they really should have been Karen's specials. Because what do you do with me? I'm a behind-the-scenes guy.
—Richard (2007)

Like Perry Como, we made it sound easy. Some people thought Perry Como was not much of a singer because it's too easy, which it was. But he was born to sing. A true singer. And Karen was a true and honest-to-god singer. Before any auto-tuning or anything else, that's us. I hope that Karen's voice and the whole Carpenters sound is appreciated for just how marvelous it is.
—Richard (2017)

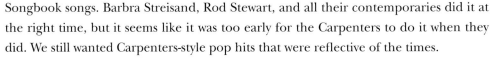

On tour, late 1975.

Songbook songs. Barbra Streisand, Rod Stewart, and all their contemporaries did it at the right time, but it seems like it was too early for the Carpenters to do it when they did. We still wanted Carpenters-style pop hits that were reflective of the times.

LEVITIN: This is fascinating to me. I'm so glad you shared this. I've never heard it put that way. I have a different but perhaps compatible perspective on this. All throughout the 1960s and the first part of the 1970s, you could still hear hits by the old guard on Top 40 radio. You could hear Frank Sinatra doing "It Was a Very Good Year" or Peggy Lee doing "Is That All There Is?" The old guard were part of the charts and played alongside Jimi Hendrix, Hamilton, Joe Frank and Reynolds, and Herb Alpert. The songs from the first few Carpenters albums were coexisting in this kind of heterogeneous landscape, which was a nice mixture of American music.

Given the interviews Karen and Richard did and their perspective on music, I always felt they aspired to be part of the establishment. They wanted to be taken seriously alongside Perry Como, Frank Sinatra, and Ella Fitzgerald. That's why you see them in specials with Ella and Perry. That's what they wanted to be.

PANCOAST: I agree with you except that I feel that we have definitive evidence that Karen would have been doing more contemporary music. We have her solo album. Those were songs she selected, and they were anything but standards. I'm just not sure that Karen aspired to the same things that Richard did.

LEVITIN: Fair enough. I keep saying "they."

SCHMIDT: *As Time Goes By* **was first released in Japan with a hidden bonus track, "And When He Smiles." For the US release, the song was given its own track. There's such an innocent sense of optimism in her voice here. What are your thoughts on this song?**

PANCOAST: One of my first thoughts about this song was that it *had* to have been written about a woman originally. You know what was the dead giveaway? The "doesn't have a point of view" lyric. I was listening to it and said, "What? Who would write a song about a *guy* who didn't have a point of view in those days?"

MILLER: Imagine if Juliet had sung a song to Romeo, it might have been this song. It just seems innocent and youthful. They're singing about smiles and sunshine and happiness and rainbows. Karen's pure voice always comes through when there's an element of simplicity to a song like this.

ABOUT THE COMMENTATORS

Mx Justin Vivian Bond is a trans-genre artist living in New York City. As a performer both on and Off-Broadway, Mx Bond has received numerous accolades, winning an Obie (2001), a Bessie (2004), a Tony nomination (2007), the Ethyl Eichelberger Award (2007), the Peter Reed Foundation Grant, and a Foundation for Contemporary Arts Grants to Artists Award. V is the author of the Lambda Literary Award–winning memoir *TANGO: My Childhood, Backwards and in High Heels* (Feminist Press, 2011).

Born in Saskatchewan, Canada, **Michelle Berting Brett** has enjoyed performing all over the world in musical theatre, as a cabaret/jazz and recording artist, and as a teacher and adjudicator. Since 2009 Michelle has toured North America as lead vocalist (and coproducer with her husband, Mark Brett) of two shows celebrating the Carpenters' legacy: *We've Only Just Begun: Carpenters Remembered* and *Merry Christmas Darling: Carpenters' Christmas*.

Described as "heavenly" (*New York Times*) and "wonderful, striking," with "essayistic songs about female revenge and politics" (Hilton Als, *Paris Review*), **Nath Ann Carrera** has had solo shows at La MaMa, Joe's Pub, Wild Project, and the Afterglow Festival, sings as Witch Camp with Amber Martin, performs with Justin Vivian Bond, opened for Martha Wainwright at City Winery, and has sung at P.S. 122, The Kitchen, Abrons Arts Center, Le Poisson Rouge, SFMOMA, MoMA PS1, Lincoln Center, and the Kennedy Center.

Inspired by Richard Carpenter to study music, **Jeffrey de Hart** worked in A&R and business affairs at Sony Music (Relativity, RED & TriStar, 1994–1999). He produced *ABBA–A Tribute: The 25th Anniversary Celebration* (Repeat, 1999), was a Swedish correspondent for *Billboard* (2000–2007) and provided research and wrote liner notes for the six-CD box set *Agnetha Fältskog De Första Åren 1967–1979* (Sony, 2004).

Mary Edwards is a composer whose projects range from recordings described as "evocative of epic cinematic scores combined with lyrical intimacy" (*Time Out*) to immersive environmental and architectural sound installations praised as "evocative and engaging" (*Bedford Standard-Times*). Themes of temporality, impermanence, nostalgia, 1960s/70s-era film soundtracks, Mid-Century Modernism, and the natural world are interspersed throughout her work. Her discography includes the forthcoming *Natural Anthem, Endeavour: A Space Trilogy for the NASA Expedition of Dr. Mae C. Jemison*, and *Everyday Until Tomorrow*, an homage to JFK Airport and the opulence of early air travel.

A devout Carpenters fan, **Gina Garan** is a doll designer and photographer. She has published nearly a dozen books of her work, including *This Is Blythe* and *Susie Says*, a collaboration with downtown superstar Justin Vivian Bond. Her photos have been displayed in solo shows and group shows around the world. Garan has designed and produced several new dolls, including ginagirls, Bendel's Girls, and Vladonna, and her Susie Says doll line will be available in 2019. Gina is also the founder of mybestjudy, an agency that caters to drag performers. She lives in Williamsburg, Brooklyn, with Carpenter, her aptly named teenage son.

Anyone who ever donned legwarmers remembers **Cynthia Gibb** as one of the stars of the TV series *Fame!* She has over sixty film, TV, and theater credits and received a Golden Globe nomination for her portrayal of Gypsy Rose Lee in *Gypsy*, opposite Bette Midler. She also starred in the 1989 TV movie *The Karen Carpenter Story*. With over forty years professional experience as an actress, singer, and dancer, she is a member of the prestigious Actors' Studio and has taught hundreds of singing and acting students in Connecticut, Los Angeles, and in master classes across Italy.

British singer/songwriter **Harriet** is known for her distinctive sound and passion for music from the '60s and '70s. Her first original song, "Afterglow," was added to Soundcloud in 2014 and released on her debut album produced by Steve Anderson and featuring the Royal Philharmonic Orchestra two years later. Her original Christmas song, "Maybe This Christmas," caught the attention of BBC Radio 2, and they continue to champion her work and expand her fan base. Frequently compared to Karen Carpenter, Harriet's sound strongly resembles the music she grew up on, which includes Carole King, Bread, and the Beatles.

With an unrivaled passion for pop music preservation and study, **Quentin Harrison** has spent over a decade writing about its history, using a variety of formats to reach readers. Harrison's works have appeared in various reissued CDs and online music review outlets. He has published four books from his fourteen-book *Record Redux* series, which examines the discographies of female musicians including the Spice Girls, Carly Simon, Donna Summer, and Madonna.

Doug Haverty has worked in the entertainment business for over forty years as a graphic designer, merchandiser, publicist, and marketer for several record companies, including A&M Records. He has designed the packaging for more than 400 releases from Universal, Warner Brothers, and EMI (soundtracks, cast albums, jazz, and pop). He has supplied graphics for numerous theatre organizations, the Los Angeles Jazz Society, The Thalians, Associated Television International, LAPD, LAFD, and the Grammys as well as designed baseball cards for Weird Al Yankovic and codesigned the coffee table book: *The Ukulele: A Visual History*. As an author, his award-winning plays and musicals have been published and produced around the world.

Drew Jansen has a enjoyed an active and varied career as a musical composer/lyricist (*Church Basement Ladies, How to Talk Minnesotan: The Musical*, among many others), television writer (*Mystery Science Theater 3000*), and performer (*Let's Bowl!*), voice-over and on-camera host (numerous commercial and industrial endeavors nationwide), freelance copywriter for greeting cards and comic strips, and cabaret pianist and singer. Jansen is the keyboardist, background vocalist, and music director for *Close to You: The Music of the Carpenters*.

Richard Tyler Jordan is the author of twelve books, perhaps most notably *The Polly Pepper Mysteries*, as well as the nonfiction work, *"But Darling, I'm Your Auntie Mame!"* He was a senior publicist for thirty years in the feature film marketing division of the Walt Disney Studios. Visit him at www.amalfibooks.com. He is obsessed (in a perfectly normal way!) with the Carpenters.

Vice president at the Recording Academy/GRAMMY Awards, **David Konjoyan** coproduced *If I Were a Carpenter*, the 1994 Carpenters tribute album featuring Sheryl Crow, Dishwalla, Redd Kross, Matthew Sweet, and 4 Non Blondes. He is the editor of the book *A GRAMMY Salute to Music Legends–All-Star Artists Pay Tribute to Their Musical Heroes*.

Michael Lansing was a roadie for the Carpenters during their 1976 world tour, and served as tour manager for artists including Melissa Manchester, Leo Sayer, and Eric Carmen. During his stint as personal manager with Lippman Entertainment, Lansing worked with numerous artists, producers, and writers, including Bernie Taupin. More recently he has made a name for himself in the amusement game business, having codesigned many modern and transitional custom pool tables.

Dr. Daniel J. Levitin is emeritus professor of psychology, behavioral neuroscience, and music at McGill University in Montreal, Quebec. He is the author of several number-one bestselling books including *The World in Six Songs, The Organized Mind*, and *This Is Your Brain on Music*. He has been a consultant to A&M Records on various music reissues, as well as a consultant and writer for documentaries on the Carpenters produced for A&E and PBS. His writing has appeared in the *New York Times* and the *New Yorker*, among others.

Equally at home on the podium and at the keyboard, **Jan McDaniel** has been on the faculty of the Bass School of Music at Oklahoma City University for nearly two decades and is a professor of vocal coaching. He is also a conductor of the Oklahoma City University Opera and Musical Theater Company, having served as musical director for dozens of productions. As a collaborative pianist he has performed with such notable artists as Kelli O'Hara, Mary Jane Johnson, Susanne Mentzer, Kristin Chenoweth, Latonia Moore, Marquita Lister, Kurt Ollmann, Uwe Heilmann, Yvonne Redman, and Leona Mitchell.

Johnny Ray Miller is the author of *When We're Singin': The Partridge Family & Their Music* and was a consultant and contributor for the A&E *Biography* special on David Cassidy. He has a thirty-year history of producing, directing, acting, and managing live theatre and has promoted concerts for David Cassidy, Davy Jones, and others. Miller also teaches theatre and acting to students of all ages.

Author, biographer, and journalist **Tom Nolan** grew up in Los Angeles, was a busy child actor in the 1950s and early 1960s, and began writing for the *Los Angeles Times* magazine *West* in 1966. Nolan penned the 1974 *Rolling Stone* cover story on the Carpenters, "Up from Downey," interviewed Karen and Richard for *Compendium* (an in-house publication of A&M Records), and wrote the liner notes for their 1977 *Passage* album.

Ted Ottaviano was signed as an artist/composer to the Warner Music Group from 1986 to 1996 and was a founding member of the group Book of Love. The band released five albums, had over a dozen Top 10 Dance Singles, and in 2016 released *MMXVI: The 30th Anniversary Collection*. Ted was named a presidential fellow in 2010 by CASE Western Reserve University for teaching Electro Pop: The History of Popular Electronic Music, a course developed with the Rock and Roll Hall of Fame. He continues to lecture and teach at schools including New York University and Emory University.

A lifelong Carpenters fan, **Judy Pancoast** is a singer, songwriter, and recording artist whose *Weird Things Are Everywhere!* was nominated for the 2011 Grammy Award nomination for Best Children's Album. She is also known for her infectious Christmas hit, "The House on Christmas Street," which can be heard each Christmas season on radio stations across the country. In addition to her concerts for children and families, Judy performs a cabaret show entitled "All My Best Memories: Built by the Carpenters," which has had several successful performances at New York renowned Don't Tell Mama cabaret.

In his teens, **Mike Ragogna** was developed as a singer-songwriter by producers Terry Cashman and Tommy West. He wrote and recorded jingles, penned the country hit "Slow Boat to China," and his songs were featured on projects like the *Roar* soundtrack and *Spider-Man: Rock Reflections of a Superhero*. Mike recorded seven albums, his video duet with Dobie Gray, "Home," premiering on the *Huffington Post* for which Mike later blogged. He wrote liner notes and worked for labels EMI, Universal, BMG, and Razor & Tie, producing projects for acts ranging from Joni Mitchell and Aerosmith to Sublime and D'Angelo.

Rumer is the award-winning British pop singer/songwriter *Q Magazine* calls the "heir to Dusty Springfield and Karen Carpenter." Her 2010 debut album *Seasons of My Soul* (2010) sold over a million copies worldwide and since then she has released *Boys Don't Cry*, *Into Colour*, and *This Girl's in Love: A Bacharach & David Songbook*, the latter a collaboration with her musical (and life) partner, Rob Shirakbari. She has sold out concert halls around the world and performed for the queen of England at Buckingham Palace and President Barack Obama at the White House.

Joel Samberg is an author, journalist, playwright, and corporate communications writer. He has published four books, including *Some Kind of Lonely Clown: The Music, Memory, and Melancholy Lives of Karen Carpenter* (BearManor Media) and *Reel Jewish: A Century of Jewish*

Movies (Jonathan David). He has also published articles in *Hartford Magazine, Pittsburgh Magazine, New Jersey Monthly,* and many others.

Rob Shirakbari is the longtime music director, keyboardist, and arranger for both Dionne Warwick and Burt Bacharach, as well as the producer/composer partner to Rumer. He has recorded and performed with such legendary artists as Adele, Elvis Costello, Sir Elton John, Stevie Wonder, Sheryl Crow, Whitney Houston, Chrissie Hynde, Ray Charles, Faith Hill, Wynonna, Aretha Franklin, Michael Bublé, Gladys Knight, Frank Sinatra, Queen Latifah, David Foster, Gloria Estefan, Barry Manilow, Cyndi Lauper, Olivia Newton-John, Patti LaBelle, Smokey Robinson, Johnny Mathis, and Natalie Cole. As a writer, Rob is a longtime contributor to *Keyboard* and *Electronic Musician* magazines.

Tom Smucker grew up in Chicago and has lived in New York City since 1967. He's written about pop music and politics in publications such as *Creem, Fusion,* and the *Village Voice.* Tom's latest book is *Why the Beach Boys Matter,* published by the University of Texas Press in 2018. Much of his writing over the decades is available at www.tomsmucker.org.

Paul Steinberg is a writer, journalist, and public health specialist who leads London's HIV Prevention Program and is a regular commentator in the media on a variety of issues related to health and campaigns. Previously he was a journalist at the BBC and wrote for various magazines and print titles, including regular pieces about the Carpenters and their music. He studied at the Universities of Sheffield, Sussex and Birkbeck College, London.

Houston Grand Opera artistic and music director **Patrick Summers** has conducted more than sixty operas since he joined the company in 1998. Some highlights include conducting the company's first-ever complete cycle of Wagner's *Ring* and its first performances of the Verdi Requiem. Maestro Summers has enjoyed a long association with San Francisco Opera (SFO) and was honored in 2015 with the San Francisco Opera Medal. His work with SFO includes conducting Jake Heggie's *Moby-Dick,* which was recorded and telecast on PBS's *Great Performances.* In 2017, he was awarded an honorary doctor of music degree from Indiana University.

A fan of Karen and Richard since first hearing "We've Only Just Begun" in 1970, **Mark Taft** saw the Carpenters perform live in Las Vegas during their 1976 tour and had the pleasure of meeting them backstage. Taft is the founder of the *Insights and Sounds* blog and considers the *Horizon* album as the collection that best showcases the duo's incredible talents. He is an international tour guide, husband, father, and grandfather and resides in Colorado.

Chris Tassin is a New Orleans native known for his portraits and pop art. His work is loved by Carpenters enthusiasts from around the world and was featured in *Little Girl Blue: The Life of Karen Carpenter.* Tassin also created and produced the "Punchy Players" comedy web series, which brought classic Hollywood personalities into everyday situations.

New Jersey native **Dena Tauriello** is a drummer, educator, and author, best known for her work with Antigone Rising, an all-female rock band. She fell in love the notion of becoming a drummer after seeing the Carpenters perform and meeting Karen Carpenter backstage. Tauriello has been a full-time professional drummer since 2002 and currently works with Rob Thomas of Matchbox 20 and on the Broadway musical *Head Over Heels.* She is also a freelance writer for *Modern Drummer* magazine and authored a feature on Karen Carpenter for the publication. For more information, visit denatauriello.com.

Gary Theroux is an Emmy-nominated and multiple *Billboard,* Telly, Golden Reel, Communicator, and New York Festivals award winner for clients ranging from Disney to PBS. Among his productions are "Legends of Comedy," "100 Greatest Christmas Hits of All Time" and "History of Rock 'n' Roll." As music and entertainment editor for *Reader's Digest*, Theroux directed the production of *Carpenters: Their Greatest Hits and Finest Performances*, featuring an in-depth interview with Karen and Richard. A longtime radio programmer, DJ, entertainment historian, UCLA instructor, and author, he is currently completing the TV documentary *Inside the History of Rock 'n Roll*.

Karen Tongson is the author of *Relocations: Queer Suburban Imaginaries* (2011) and *Why Karen Carpenter Matters* (2019). She is associate professor of English, gender, and sexuality studies and American studies and ethnicity at USC. Her writing and cultural commentary have appeared in numerous public and scholarly venues. *Postmillennial Pop*, the award-winning book series she coedits with Henry Jenkins at NYU Press, has published over twenty titles. You can also hear Karen talk about pop culture, the arts, and entertainment on the weekly *Pop Rocket* podcast, hosted by comedian Guy Branum.

From the age of thirteen, **Matt Wallace** played in bands influenced by Black Sabbath and Deep Purple, but he was an avid fan of Top 40 radio and the Carpenters, too. Wallace recorded several bands in the San Francisco Bay area, which eventually led to working with Faith No More. He later coproduced *If I Were a Carpenter*, the 1994 Carpenters tribute album featuring Sheryl Crow, Dishwalla, Redd Kross, Matthew Sweet, and 4 Non Blondes. Wallace has since worked with Maroon 5, the Replacements, Hoobastank, and Andy Grammer.

ABOUT THE AUTHOR

Randy L. Schmidt is the author of the critically acclaimed *Little Girl Blue: The Life of Karen Carpenter*, a *New York Times* Editor's Choice and *Wall Street Journal* bestseller. His latest publication is *Dolly on Dolly: Interviews and Encounters with Dolly Parton*, a title in the *Musicians in Their Own Words* series from Chicago Review Press. He also compiled and edited *Yesterday Once More: The Carpenters Reader* and *Judy Garland on Judy Garland: Interviews and Encounters*. Schmidt has served as creative consultant for several television documentaries on the Carpenters, including the *E! True Hollywood Story*, A&E's *Biography*, and VH1's *Behind the Music*. More recently, he contributed to *Karen Carpenter: Goodbye to Love* and *Autopsy: The Last Hours of Karen Carpenter*, both produced for ITV in the United Kingdom and Reelz TV in the United States. A music educator for more than twenty years, Schmidt teaches elementary music in Denton, Texas.

PHOTO CREDITS

A = All; B = Bottom; T = Top

A&M Records: p6, p36, p133, p161, p170. **ABC-TV:** p98A, p170. **Alamy Stock Photos:** Barry King, p138; Jeffrey Mayer/Pictorial Press Ltd, p165; Moviestore Collection Ltd, p147; PA Images, p113; Phil Roach/Globe Photos/ZUMAPRESS.com, p20, p108; Pictorial Press Ltd, p97, p114; Ronald Grant Archive, p28T. **Archive Images:** p3, p10, p13, p23, p28B, p31, p32, p37, p43, p45, p48, p49, p53, p82, p111. **Camera Press:** Heilemann/Camera Press/Redux, p95. **Carolyn Arzac:** p104, p110, p129. **Sherry Rayn Barnett:** p40, p62, p63. **Ken Bertwell:** p52B. **Peter Borsari Archive:** viii, p24B, p33, p35, p38A, p59B, p78, p88, p89, p90, p91, p93, p109A, p124, p153. **Ed Caraeff/Iconic Images:** endpapers, i, iv-v, p55, p56A, p57A, p58, p65, p66, p67, p69, p71, p72A, p73, p74, p77, p79A, p81A, p127, p141, p149, p167, p172, p174, p175. **John Engstead/mptvimages.com:** vi, p107. **The Everett Collection:** p4, p14; Mirrorpix, p80. **Maria Luisa Galeazzi:** p39, p52T. **Leo Hetzel:** p100. **Imagecollect:** Bob Kates/Globe Photos, p135; Gary Merrin/Globe Photos, p85; Globe Photos, p24T, p27, p42 p59T, p94. **Harry Langdon:** p87, p93, p99 (colorizations by Chris Tassin). **Ambrose Martin:** p162. **Bob Merlis:** p9. **Claude Mougin:** p125, p151, p154. **Frank Pooler Collection:** p18, p19, p51. **National Archives:** p. 47. **Karen Ramone Collection:** p142. **Randy Schmidt:** p123B. **Rex/Shutterstock:** Bei, p123T; Globe Photos, p25; Andre Csillag, p84; Associated Newspapers, p101; Lennox Mclendon/AP, p118. **Bonnie Schiffman:** p159. **Norman Seeff:** ii, p117, p144.

ACKNOWLEDGMENTS

The author gratefully acknowledges Paul Ashurst, executive publisher. This book would not have been possible without his encouragement, guidance, and support. Heartfelt gratitude is also extended to the commentators for their efforts and the insight that went into the discussions contained herein. Thanks also to Laura Adam, Sue Gustin, Robert Ingves, Greg Kuritz, Chris May, Leslie Pfenninger, Jaime Rodriguez-Schmidt, Camryn Schmidt, Kaylee Schmidt, and Jen Strauch.

Special thanks to those who generously opened their collections to share images and memorabilia for this project: Paul Ashurst, Maggie Baker, Ken Bertwell, Ron Bunt, Tim Burke, Nick Butler, Tommy Carrigan, Peter Dawe, Donnie Demers, Joe DiMaria, Brenda Ehly, Tony Elflain, Hiromi Hirahata, Mary Jennings, Matthew Lambrecht, Vinnie Metzger, John P. Noel, Pam Quiggle, Marijke Siemensma, Chris Tassin, Vickie VanArtsdalen, Cindy Williams, Simon Worsley, and all the rest.

INDEX

www.mascotbooks.com

A Paul Ashurst Publication

Executive Publisher: Paul Ashurst
Cover and Book Design: Brad Norr Design
Transcriptions: Laura Adam
Editor: Michelle Williams
Photo Research: Peter Dawe
Photo Restoration: Chris Tassin
Additional Photography: Camryn Schmidt

On the front cover: Ed Caraeff (RGR Collection/Alamy Stock Photo)
On the back cover: Laurens van Houten (Pictorial Press Ltd/Alamy Stock Photo)
Page i: Las Vegas, 1974.
Page ii: Photographed by Norman Seeff in Hollywood, February 22, 1981.
Page iv-v: An outtake from the *Horizon* photo sessions.
Page vi: *Made in America* photo session outtake, March 13, 1981.
Endpapers: At A&M Studios during the *Horizon* sessions, 1975.

This book is not associated with or endorsed by Richard Carpenter, the Carpenters, their estates, or any affiliated organizations.

For more information, please contact:
Mascot Books, Inc.
620 Herndon Parkway #320
Herndon, VA 20170
info@mascotbooks.com

Library of Congress Control Number: 2018914932

CPSIA Code: PRTWP0219A
ISBN-13: 978-1-64307-321-7

Printed in Malaysia